Exploring Esther:

Serving the unseen God

© Day One Publications 2005
First printed 2005

ISBN 1-84625-010-2

9 781846 250101 >

Published by Day One Publications
Ryelands Road, Leominster, HR6 8NZ
☎ 01568 613 740 FAX 01568 611 473
email—sales@dayone.co.uk
web site—www.dayone.co.uk
North American—e-mail—sales@dayonebookstore.com
North American—web site—www.dayonebookstore.com

Designed by Steve Devane and printed by Gutenberg Press, Malta

Dedication

To my wife Chris, whose love, prayer and practical support are a cherished gift from God.

Contents

The book of Esther is a beautiful yet difficult part of the Bible. Colin Jones' magnificent exposition helps us to understand the text, resolve the complexities, and appreciate the plan of God as it unfolded within the pages of this book. He shows us how the events in Esther's life are part of God's plan and how they encourage us to live the Christian life more effectively. It is essential reading for anyone who wants to delve more deeply into this wonderful book God has given to us.

Simon J Robinson

Commendation

Very few modern commentaries on the Book of Esther manage to combine a high view of God's providence and the historicity of the narrative with serious exposition and masses of warm, practical application. This one does.

Jonathan Stephen
Director, Affinity

'Tell them a story' is what I am sometimes asked to do when I preach in small churches in the outlying areas of the Greek countryside. The village people like stories because they can quickly become caught up in a tale that is well told, and its meaning can quite easily be brought out. Around one third of the Bible is in narrative form and Jesus used stories—his parables—to great effect.

This Bible book of Esther is almost hidden away in the middle of the Old Testament and, as a result, many people merely think of it as an interesting part of Israel's history. Colin D Jones encourages us to see that there is much more. He tells the story of Esther well, outlining the events concerning this remarkable Queen with great clarity and wisdom. However, we are not only told the story; we are enabled to understand the meaning it had for its first readers and also what God is saying to us today.

By picking up this book and reading it, you will discover that there is very much more to it than dry history; it tells of our sovereign God at work even when most of the characters involved are unaware of his presence. They do not know about his activity because his name is never mentioned, nor is the activity of prayer referred to. Yet both God and his people's intercession are at the heart of this bible book.

Esther—Serving the Unseen God is not only brimming with good things, but is very easy to read as well. The text is divided into short sections with each one carrying a striking title like, 'A Brilliant Idea', 'Esther's Secret' or 'Missed Opportunities'. The Cast List near the beginning of the book helps the reader to follow the flow of the events and the helpful, concise comments direct us to consider the implication of numerous subjects such as the use of alcohol, choosing a wife (or husband), racial conflict, justice and mercy, special prayer, horoscopes, and the cost of discipleship.

Rather than ending each chapter with questions for discussion, we are also presented with subjects for reflection. This is especially helpful to those who are reading this book on their own instead of in a Bible study group. The book also contains useful charts and diagrams.

When I am writing on (or preaching) from the Old Testament, I constantly ask myself, 'How much have I mentioned the cross?' This book does not fail in this respect. While nothing is taught here that does not arise directly from the text of the Scriptures, the redemption that is ours through the atoning death and resurrection of the Lord Jesus Christ is at the crux of this work, as is the providence of God im all things.

May huge numbers of people who read this book find themselves being directed back to the Lord Jesus Christ again and again.

Michael Bentley
Bracknell, Berkshire, England

NIV	New International Version
NKJV	New King James Version
KJV	King James Version
NASB	New American Standard Bible

Introduction

The hidden God

The book of Esther is in many ways an anomaly:

- No book in the Bible speaks more clearly to us of the gracious, sovereign protection of God towards his people—yet his name is never mentioned.
- Throughout this book the invisible God can only be seen by his footprints in history. The hand that shields his people can only be perceived by faith.
- No book has more to teach us about prayer. We learn so much about the method and manner of true intercession. We see a clear foreshadowing of Christ's High Priestly office. Yet no prayer is recorded or reported.
- This lack of obvious 'religious' content has led many, even the great Reformer, Martin Luther, to seek to deny Esther a place in the canon of Scripture. The church fathers did not bother to write even one commentary on Esther between them.

The Persian Empire

The Persian Empire was the largest the world had ever seen. It covered modern-day Turkey, Iraq, Iran, Pakistan, Jordan, Lebanon, Israel, and parts of Egypt, Sudan, Libya, and Arabia. Millions of people speaking a multitude of languages all owed allegiance to their sovereign lord the king. He was known as 'The Great King, the King of Kings'.

His empire was administered by a massive bureaucracy served by a kind of 'pony express' designed to convey official paperwork from one end of the known world to the other in the shortest possible time.

It was remarkably cohesive and governed by a uniform set of laws. The official edicts passed by the king under royal seal were irrevocable.

The setting

SUSA—CAPITAL OF THE WORLD

The importance of this great city during the time of Esther is well documented by archaeologists and historians alike:

Susa (Shush), in southwestern Iran, was the ancient capital of the Elamites, an administrative center and royal residence under the Achaemenids and the eastern terminus of the Persian Royal Road that ran westward to Lydian Sardis, about 2,575 km (1,600 miles) away. Following the conquests of Alexander the Great, Susa was made a Greek colonial city-state called Seleucia-on-the-Eulaeus; it continued to flourish as a trade center through the Parthian and Sassanian periods, until its capture (AD c.640) by Islamic forces.

Rediscovered in 1850, Susa has been under almost continuous excavation by French archaeologists since 1897. Although occupation levels date back to Neolithic times (c.4000 BC), the principal objects of interest at the site are four large mounds representing the citadel, the palace of Darius I (r. 521–486 BC), and two sections of the ancient city. Significant finds at Susa have included early painted pottery and seals, proto-Elamite writing, an extensive Parthian cemetery, and the famous stele of Hammurabi bearing his law code.[1]

You can locate Susa on the map in Appendix 2 at the end of this book.

The Cast
The major characters in the book of Esther in order of appearance

KING XERXES
There were three Persian kings who bore this name. The king mentioned in the book of Esther is Xerxes I., also known as Ahasuerus.[2] He is remembered by history for launching his spectacular invasion of Greece:

Xerxes became king of Persia at the death of his father Darius the Great in 485, at a time when his father was preparing a new expedition against Greece. Xerxes finally decided to pursue the project of his father to subdue Greece, but made lengthy preparations. The expedition was ready to move in the spring of 480 and Xerxes himself took the lead. Herodotus[3] gives us a colourful description of the Persian army that he evaluates at close to two million men and about twelve hundred ships.[4] This campaign included the famous battle of Thermopylae, where 300 Spartans laid down their lives for Greece.[5]

Their valour is immortalised in legend, film and poetry. The poet A.E. Housman wrote:

The King with half the East at heel is marched from lands of morning;
Their fighters drink the rivers up, their shafts benight the air.
And he that stands will die for nought, and home there's no returning.
The Spartans on the sea-wet rock sat down and combed their hair.[6]

Scripture pictures him as a weak man. Manipulated by others [3:8–11], he is proud and self-indulgent [1:4–8], given to fits of temper and rash decisions that he later regrets [1:12, 2:1]. This is the man whom Esther must marry.

QUEEN VASHTI

Her name means 'beautiful'.[7]

As the book opens she is the queen. She is almost immediately deposed and ostracised, however, for disobeying Xerxes' command to appear for the entertainment of his drunken guests.

The person and role of Vashti have caused great controversy among modern Jews. To some she is a 'feminist hero': 'Vashti has become one of the favourite heroines of the Jewish feminist movement. This much-maligned queen, the argument goes, should be appreciated as a positive role model, a woman who dared to disregard a royal decree that would have her displayed as a sex object before King Ahashverosh's[8] rowdy drinking companions.'[9] To others she is a villain: 'There was no heroism here. There was only arrogance.'[10]

Scripture allows us to judge her action as 'right' while leaving the matter of her motives, as so often, a mystery known only to God. A Jewish tradition holds that she was the 'great-granddaughter of the arch-villain Nebuchadnezzar King of Babylon',[11] however, the Scriptures are silent as to her lineage. The inability of scholars to identify her from extant Persian records is not at all surprising; such disgrace as hers was often accompanied by the expunging of the criminal's name from all official records.

MEMUCAN

His name means 'dignified'.[12]

One in the inner circle of seven advisors to Xerxes [1:14], it was on his suggestion that Queen Vashti was deposed [1:16]. He feared that her example in disobeying the king would foment revolt among the other women of the empire [1:18]. His 'dignity' was greatly disturbed by such a prospect.

MORDECAI

His name means 'little man' or 'worshipper of Mars'.[13]

Though the latter may have been one meaning of his name, nothing could have been further from the truth. His godly character and faith shine through the story. Scripture reveals him as a man of compassion [2:7], prudence [2:10], integrity [2:22], discernment [3:2], spirituality [4:1], wisdom [4:8] and faith [4:14]. Unlike his implacable enemy Haman, he is not motivated by greed and ambition, neither is he cruel and vindictive. All his actions are dictated by one great purpose—to preserve the people of God from destruction. He may or may not have earned his name by being 'little' in physical stature, but he ranks as a spiritual giant and well deserves his place among the great heroes of the Bible.

ESTHER

Esther has two alternate names; she is introduced to us first by her Jewish name Hadassah which means 'Myrtle'. Throughout the remainder of the book, however, she is referred to by her Persian name Esther which means 'Star'.

It has always been common for 'immigrants' to blend into the host society by adopting some of its labels and customs while retaining their 'ethnic identity'. By this means they preserve something of the language and culture of 'home'. You would not have to search far in our modern multi-cultural world to find parallels. No matter how long they had been settled in Susa, the majority population would still regard Esther and Mordecai as foreigners. Sadly, she would have known all the prejudice, discrimination and injustice that seem to go with the territory. One of the undoubted glories of the church of the Lord Jesus Christ is that wherever the gospel is understood and embraced a radically alternate society springs into being. Nationality, colour, social status and all other causes of division are swept aside by the sheer joy of being 'in Christ'. Galatians 3:27–28 declares that 'All of you who were baptised into Christ have clothed yourselves with Christ. There is neither Jew nor Greek, slave nor free, male nor female, for you are all one in Christ Jesus.'

The enemies of the early church called them a 'third race'. Sadly it was intended as an insult rather than a compliment. Tertullian[14] comments, with no small degree of irony, 'We are indeed said to be the "third race" of men. What, a dog-faced race? ... Now, if they who belong to the third race are so monstrous, what must they be supposed to be who preceded them in the first and the second place?'

Before we meet her Esther has already tasted her share of sorrow. She is an orphan who has been reared and cared for by her cousin Mordecai [2:7]. If Mordecai is our hero then undoubtedly Esther is our heroine. So critical is the role played by this young woman in the unfolding drama, that the book will bear her name and she will gain everlasting fame. She is, by any standards, a remarkable woman, and richly endowed by God. She has a beauty that can capture the heart of a king [2:17]. Her attractiveness, however, is not merely physical. She possesses a character that endears her to all she meets [2:9, 15]. She is modest [2:15], dutiful [2:10], intelligent [4:11], courageous and, above all, devout [4:16]. It is difficult to imagine a young woman who better fits the biblical ideal set out by the Apostle Paul in 1 Timothy 2:9–10:

'I also want women to dress modestly, with decency and propriety, not with braided hair or gold or pearls or expensive clothes, but with good deeds, appropriate for women who profess to worship God.'

HEGAI

The meaning of his name is unknown. He was the eunuch who was charged with Esther's care when she entered the king's harem. He is the first of many servants of King Xerxes whose affection was won by Esther. A eunuch was 'primarily and literally, an emasculated man (Deut. 23:1). The Hebrew word *caric* seems, however, to have acquired a figurative meaning, which is reflected in English versions of the Bible where 'officer' and 'chamberlain' are found as renderings (compare Gen. 37:36, 39:1) and where *caric* is applied to married men [4:4]. The barbarous practice of self-mutilation and the mutilation of others in this way was prevalent throughout the Orient.'[15]

BIGTHANA AND TERESH

Bigthana means 'in their wine-press';[16] Teresh means 'strictness'.[17]

These two men were honoured with prestigious service as personal bodyguards to King Xerxes. Some issue, real or imagined, caused them to become dissatisfied and angry. Lacking integrity, they planned the assassination of their king. In the providence of God, Mordecai discovered their plot and (through Esther) alerted King Xerxes. The king is saved, the villains dispatched but no reward forthcoming for Mordecai. Xerxes' initial lack of gratitude is later to prove crucial in the overthrow of Haman and the deliverance of the Jews.

HAMAN THE AGAGITE

His name means 'magnificent'[18] and that certainly reflected his self-perception. He is motivated by pride and anger [3:5]; he is manipulative [3:8], callous and cruel [3:13; 5:14]. Like many such men he is ultimately a coward of the worst sort [7:7]. His meteoric rise to pre-eminence is followed by an even more spectacular fall.

There are differences of opinion on his designation as an 'Agagite'. The Targum[19] and Josephus[20] interpret the description of him—the Agagite—as signifying that he was of Amalekitish descent. The Jews hiss whenever his name is mentioned on the day of Purim.[21] If this linkage is correct then he is a direct descendant of King Agag (1 Sam. 15). Saul's disobedience in sparing this man despite God's express command caused him to forfeit his kingdom. Many modern expositors make this connection. American preacher and author John McArthur says, 'Because of his lineage from Agag, Haman carried deep hostility toward the Jews.'[22] Warren Wiersbe comments, 'Haman was a descendant of the Amalekites, the archenemies of the Jews'.[23] Many older writers, such as Matthew Henry, also share this view.[24] Certainly, family and racial hatred can endure through the centuries and motivate one generation to seek revenge for ancient wrongs. We need to guard against the deep roots that bitterness thrusts into the fertile soil of men's hearts. How we should heed the advice of the Apostle Paul and the writer to the Hebrews: 'Get rid of all bitterness, rage and anger, brawling and slander, along with every form of malice. Be kind and compassionate to one another, forgiving each other, just as in Christ God forgave you' (Eph.4:31–32). 'See to it that no one misses the grace of God and that no bitter root grows up to cause trouble and defile many' (Heb.12:15).

ZERESH

The wife of Haman whose name, appropriately enough, means 'gold',[25] something which, along with its close companion power, her husband dearly loved [5:11]. Like Jezebel (1 Kings 21), she provoked her husband to commit great evil [5:14].

Notes

1 http://www.parspage.com/history/cities.htm

2 *Nelson's Illustrated Bible Dictionary,* (Nashville, TN: Thomas Nelson Publishers, 1986), p. 1111.

3 *Histories,* VII, 59–100.

4 http://plato-dialogues.org/tools/char/xerxes.htm

5 **Kevin Hendryx,** see http://uts.cc.utexas.edu/~sparta/topics/alamo.htm

6 http://www.kalliope.org/ffront.cgi?fhandle=housman (1859–1936).

7 2060 in *Enhanced Strong's Lexicon.*

8 An alternate spelling of Ahasuerus rendered in modern translations as Xerxes.

9 http://www.ucalgary.ca/~elsegal/Shokel/910301_Vashti.html

10 http://www.aish.com/holidays/purim/villainy_of_vashti.asp

11 http://www.ucalgary.ca/~elsegal/Shokel/910301_Vashti.html

12 4462 in *Enhanced Strong's Lexicon.*

13 4782 in *Enhanced Strong's Lexicon.*

14 http://www.earlychristianwritings.com/text/tertullian06.html

15 *International Standard Bible Encyclopaedia,* Biblesoft, Electronic Database Copyright 1996.

16 904 in *Enhanced Strong's Lexicon*

17 575 in *Enhanced Strong's Lexicon.*

18 2001 in *Enhanced Strong's Lexicon.*

19 The Targum is the translation of the Old Testament from the Hebrew language into Aramaic. The word means 'translation'.

20 A Jewish historian, who was born AD 37/38, and died early in the second century. Author among other works of *History of the Jewish War* and *Jewish Antiquities*

21 W. Smith, *Smith's Bible Dictionary* (electronic ed. of the revised ed.) (Nashville, TN: Thomas Nelson).

22 J.J. MacArthur, *The MacArthur Study Bible* (electronic ed.) (Es 1:1) (Nashville, TN: Word Pub., 1997).

23 W.W, Wiersbe, *Wiersbe's expository outlines on the Old Testament* (Es 1:1) (Wheaton, IL: Victor Books, 1993).

24 Matthew Henry, *Commentary on the whole Bible: Complete and unabridged in one volume* (Es 3:1) (Peabody: Hendrickson, 1996).

25 James Orr, MA, DD, General Editor, entry for 'Zeresh', *International Standard Bible Encyclopedia,* http://www.studylight.org/enc/isb/view.cgi?number=T9374. 1915.

The conduct of a king

Esther 1:1–11

QUEEN VASHTI DEPOSED

1 This is what happened during the time of Xerxes, the Xerxes who ruled over 127 provinces stretching from India to Cush: ²At that time King Xerxes reigned from his royal throne in the citadel of Susa, ³and in the third year of his reign he gave a banquet for all his nobles and officials. The military leaders of Persia and Media, the princes, and the nobles of the provinces were present.

4For a full 180 days he displayed the vast wealth of his kingdom and the splendour and glory of his majesty. 5When these days were over, the king gave a banquet, lasting seven days, in the enclosed garden of the king's palace, for all the people from the least to the greatest, who were in the citadel of Susa. 6The garden had hangings of white and blue linen, fastened with cords of white linen and purple material to silver rings on marble pillars. There were couches of gold and silver on a mosaic pavement of porphyry, marble, mother-of-pearl and other costly stones. 7Wine was served in goblets of gold, each one different from the other, and the royal wine was abundant, in keeping with the king's liberality. 8By the king's command each guest was allowed to drink in his own way, for the king instructed all the wine stewards to serve each man what he wished.

9Queen Vashti also gave a banquet for the women in the royal palace of King Xerxes.

10On the seventh day, when King Xerxes was in high spirits from wine, he commanded the seven eunuchs who served him—Mehuman, Biztha, Harbona, Bigtha, Abagtha, Zethar and Carcas—11to bring before him Queen Vashti, wearing her royal crown, in order to display her beauty to the people and nobles, for she was lovely to look at.

Beyond riches 1:1–3

As we saw in the Introduction, Xerxes ruled over a vast and all-powerful empire. In his own eyes his wealth and power knew no bounds. Derek Prime refers to an ancient inscription discovered in the royal palace at Persepolis:

a palace of considerable magnificence, extravagance and lavishness, archaeologists discovered a foundation stone that confirms Xerxes' titles and his territorial claims mentioned in the book of Esther. It illustrates not only the extent of his territories, but his arrogance. It begins, 'I am Xerxes, the great king, the only king, the king of [all] countries [which speak] all kind of languages, the king of this [entire] big and far-reaching earth—the son of King Darius, the Achaemenian, a Persian, son of a Persian, an Aryan of Aryan descent. Herodotus confirms the extent of Xerxes' territory. His empire was thought to be so vast that the sun never set upon it.[1]

Such grandeur often comes at the terrible price of human pride and eventual ruin. A further biblical example is Hezekiah, King of Judah, who foolishly paraded his wealth before the envoys of Babylon only to be told by the prophet Isaiah that those same treasures would be carried away by the king of Babylon as spoils of war (Isa. 39). What depth of cautionary wisdom is contained in this warning of Scripture: 'Pride goes before destruction, a haughty spirit before a fall' (Prov. 16:18).

Xerxes had numerous palaces, the chief ones being the summer stronghold in Persepolis and the winter citadel in the beautiful city of Susa. It was Susa where the events recorded in the book of Esther took place. In this third year of his reign, the entire period of royal residence was apparently given over to the entertainment of the empire's officials. This was no doubt combined with matters of state. We are not to imagine every moment of these six months being spent in drunken revelry. Almost certainly officials came and went as their duties permitted. Whatever business was conducted was done in lavish surroundings and culminated in an abundance of food and drink. It seems likely that at the end of this period the balance between work and play changed and for seven days all restraint was removed. They ate, drank and made merry as no group of men had ever done before. So impressive was this display of opulence that Scripture records even small details of the décor. Particular emphasis is laid on the removal of the normal restraints imposed by drinking etiquette. This was a literal free-for-all, with no danger here, as in Cana of the wine running out (John 2:1–3). Even the usual protocol that no one was to out-eat or out-drink the host was set aside. No greater exhibition of the wealth and generosity of their king could be imagined.

The show-off 1:4–6

This was an opulent feast by any standard. First, there was the gathering of the cream of society from the far corners of Xerxes' realm. Hundreds assembled to be treated to a mind-blowing display of luxury. No expense was spared on the surroundings, food or drink. Any father, impoverished by paying the ever-increasing expenses of a fashionable modern wedding, can at least rejoice that he was not footing this bill. The purpose was to impress, and every detail was marked by extravagance. Every individual whim was catered for. In our society we too often labour under the mistaken idea that wealth brings joy. The truth is more accurately reflected in the wisdom of Proverbs: 'He who is full loathes honey, but to the hungry even what is bitter tastes sweet' (Prov. 27:7).

Luxury, however appealing, has a habit of leaving those who seek after it empty and dissatisfied. During twenty years serving as an officiating chaplain to the Royal Air Force, I made an interesting observation. On occasions various members of the Royal Family would visit the station. The preparations were extensive and sometimes amusing. I never failed to smile at the arrival of plants, bushes and even trees which (still in their pots) were strategically buried, so that when the visit was over, they could be returned to the hire firm. One would have thought that for such an occasion the table in the mess room would be laden with rich delicacies. This was never the case, however; the food, although always cooked to perfection and presented with care, tended towards the plain and simple. I eventually learned that this occurred according to the specific instructions of the Palace. Clearly you can have too much of a good thing, and worse still, have it far too often.

The wise moderate their behaviour, but the foolish person embarks on a meaningless quest to 'top' the last experience with an even better one. Xerxes was not wise and his pride was a driving force in his extreme lavishness.

This pattern has been endlessly repeated throughout history. The Roman Caesars often sought to outdo their predecessors as they staged the 'games' in the Coliseum. Chariot races, combat to the death, full battles (even naval battles) were reconstructed. Men were pitched against exotic wild beasts. Each spectacle had to be surpassed by the next until cruelty knew no bounds in this sick spectator sport. The same spirit is evident in Hitler's Berlin Olympics or the Nuremberg rallies or the Moscow May Day parades. Powerful men need to demonstrate just how limitless they think their wealth and power really is.

An abundance of wine 1:7–8

Christians differ in their opinion as to the wisdom of consuming alcohol. Some will argue for total abstinence, others for temperance, still others that partaking is an expression of their liberty in Christ. It is a serious issue in our society where alcohol abuse is rampant. The statistics are, to say the least, sobering. Driving offences, public order issues and sexual immorality are all clearly aggravated by overindulgence.

The following come from the most recent official Government Statistics:

(A unit of alcohol is approximately equivalent to a half pint of beer, a small glass of wine or a single measure of spirits.)

- In England in 2001, almost two fifths (38%) of men had drunk more than 4 units of alcohol on at least one day in the previous week: about one fifth of women (22%) had drunk more than 3 units of alcohol on at least one day in the previous week.
- In 2001, average weekly alcohol consumption in England was 16.9 units for men and 7.5 units for women.
- In 2002, about a quarter (24%) of pupils in England aged 11–15 had drunk alcohol in the previous week:
- Provisional estimates suggest that in 2002, 6 per cent of road traffic accidents involved illegal alcohol levels, and that these accidents resulted in a total of 20,140 casualties.[2]

Alcohol is a drug and as such it is capable of decreasing our inhibitions and inflating our self-confidence. It can seriously distort our judgement. There would seem to be only two valid Christian positions on its consumption— abstinence or great moderation. Whatever our conclusion, taken to excess drinking is undeniably a pathway to disaster. So it proved for Xerxes. Searching for a new delight for his guests at the height of the feast, he decided to display yet one more of his beautiful possessions—his Queen.

Displaying the queen 1:9–11

The world of men has departed so far from the plan of God. It began long ago at the dawn of human history, in Eden itself. Man exchanged paradise for disobedience and death. The result of that first sin had immediate repercussions and set a pattern that persists to this day. Read again the historical narrative recorded in Genesis 1–3. God made man and woman as companions; Jews in particular have always stressed the significance of the fact that Eve was taken from Adam's side, as it were, under his protective wing, to be cherished, guarded and respected. That was the place God appointed for the first woman. The position of her descendants has often fallen far short of that high ideal. Too often she has been degraded, downtrodden and exploited as an object of lustful entertainment, a possession to be used and paraded. This is what Xerxes sought to make of Vashti, his queen, his wife. She was not invited to join the guests; she was summoned to please their eyes. She was to titillate the senses of a crowd of drunken men.

Xerxes had abandoned his responsibility as a king towards a subject let alone to the queen, his wife. He had failed as a king, a husband and even as a man. How true are the words of the Psalmist: 'A man who has riches without understanding is like the beasts that perish' (Ps. 49:20).

The hand of God

We have already noted in the Introduction that while the name of God is not mentioned in this book, the hand of God is seen everywhere. This is itself one of the great lessons of Esther for our own generation. Living in the United Kingdom at the beginning of the twenty-first century, it is more than likely that if we hear the Lord's name it is because it is being taken in vain. We must therefore guard against the erroneous conclusion that he is not both present and at work. When Elijah confronted the prophets of the false god Baal during their epic battle on Mount Carmel, he taunted them with their idol's silence and inactivity (1 Kings 18). The true God, however, is never deep in thought, busy, travelling or sleeping. When he is unseen it is because, as Isaiah says, 'Truly you are a God who hides himself, O God and Saviour of Israel' (Isa. 45:15).

During the long years of captivity in Egypt the Lord was seemingly silent and hidden, but he both saw and heard the need of his people and at the right time came to deliver (Exod. 3:7). So it is in the dark days of our own era—the Lord is always near. The Psalmist expresses the truth that however near our enemies may seem, God is also close at hand: 'Those who devise wicked schemes are near, but they are far from your law. Yet you are near, O Lord, and all your commands are true' (Ps. 119:150–151). He is never far from those who seek him in prayer: 'The Lord is near to all who call on him, to all who call on him in truth' (Ps.145:18).

Luke records the occasion when the Apostle Paul, a prisoner on his way to face judgement in Rome, was travelling by ship. As a violent storm swept both ship and passengers on towards certain destruction, the Lord reassured his servant of his care and sovereignty: 'The following night the Lord stood near Paul and said, "Take courage! As you have testified about me in Jerusalem, so you must also testify in Rome"' (Acts 23:11).

Throughout the book of Esther we are encouraged to see the providential dealings of God through their gracious outcomes. The foolishness of a king, the reaction of a queen, the fear of self-seeking officials are all revealed to be not haphazard events but part of a great divine plan. God is putting into place the first element of his deliverance—Esther. He does all this before anyone but he knows that there is even a problem to be solved. 'Do not be like them, for your Father knows what you need before you ask him' (Matt. 6:8). 'Before they call I will answer; while they are still speaking I will hear' (Isa. 65:24).

THE SUPREMACY OF CHRIST

Many different individuals will grace the stage of this drama before it is over. Some are mighty, others lowly. Occasionally we will seek to draw some comparisons and reflect on the supremacy of the Lord Jesus to them all.

PRIDE AND HUMILITY

Xerxes, despite his great wealth and power, was deeply insecure. He was unlikely to earn the suffix 'the Great' that had been given to his father Darius. So he set out to impress: everything he did was on a grand scale and everything was done to be seen. What a contrast with the Lord Jesus Christ, who though he was by right King of kings and Lord of lords, clothed himself with humility (1 Tim. 6:13–16, Rev. 17:14, 19:11–16).

Consider the sublime words of the Apostle Paul, written to the Christians in Philippi:

Who, being in very nature God,
did not consider equality with God something to be grasped,
but made himself nothing,
taking the very nature of a servant,
being made in human likeness.
And being found in appearance as a man,
he humbled himself
and became obedient to death—even death on a cross!
Therefore God exalted him to the highest place
and gave him the name that is above every name,
that at the name of Jesus every knee should bow,
in heaven and on earth and under the earth,
and every tongue confess that Jesus Christ is Lord,
to the glory of God the Father.

Philippians 2:6–11

AUTHORITY AND DOMINION

Xerxes is a man swept along by the tide of events. His drunken foolishness robs him of his wife. His self-seeking advisors impose their will on him. His own law ties his hands and prevents him from restoring his queen. How different is Christ! Not only the world of men but even the wind and the waves obey him (Mark 4:41). Nothing is beyond the realm of his dominion; his authority extends even to the laying down and taking up again of his own life (John 10:17–18).

THE ULTIMATE HUSBAND

Xerxes clearly fails in his duty to cherish and protect his wife Vashti. He then further compounds his guilt by punishing her when the real fault lies with him. There could be no starker contrast when we turn to look at Christ. Throughout Scripture the image of God as the husband and his people as his bride is common: 'For your Maker is your husband—the LORD Almighty is his name—the Holy One of Israel is your Redeemer; he is called the God of all the earth' (Isa. 54:5). (See also Ezekiel 16, Jeremiah 3, Hosea 2.)

In the New Testament the focus is on the relationship between Christ and his bride, the Church. This focus culminates in the book of Revelation with the wedding of the bride and the lamb (Rev. 19:7, 21:2–17). In Christ we have set before us the supreme example, the perfect husband. Ephesians 5:25–28 develops this theme at length and sets the atoning death of the Saviour in this context:

Husbands, love your wives, just as Christ loved the church and gave himself up for her to make her holy, cleansing her by the washing with water through the word, and to present her to himself as a radiant church, without stain or wrinkle or any other blemish, but holy and blameless. In this same way, husbands ought to love their wives as their own bodies. He who loves his wife loves himself.

Christ does not use the church for his own pleasure; rather he lays down his own life to ransom and redeem her. He, not Xerxes and his kind, is the model for Christian husbands.

Using the 'reflection/discussion topics'

At the end of each chapter you will find a section with this heading. If you are reading on your own, you might find it profitable to pause before reading the next chapter to think through the issues that have been raised. Where indicated, there are verses you will need to look up.

If you are using this book for group study, each member of the group will need to have read the chapter in order to get the most from the discussion. There will always be too much material to cover in a single meeting. You will need either to spend a number of weeks on each chapter or narrow the list of topics to pursue. Don't worry if members of the group are using a different version of the Bible. It is often helpful and can throw fresh light on familiar passages. At least one person should use the NIV on which the study is based.

Reflection/discussion topics from Chapter 1

1 What do you think the Christian attitude should be to wealth? Luke

8:14, 21:1–4; James 1:10–11; 1 Tim. 6:17–19.

2 *Consider* Proverbs 30:8–9 as a practical life-goal. What effect would such a choice have on your hopes and ambitions for the future?

3 To what extent do you think that the present preoccupation with 'designer labels', possessing the latest technology, etc. is a scaled-own expression of the same pride Xerxes displayed?

4 Which do you think is the wisest way for a Christian to approach the issue of alcohol?

5 What biblical principles have you used to come to your conclusion?

6 How would the biblical relationship between men and women work out in the main areas of our lives: home, work and church?

Notes

1 **Derek Prime,** *Unspoken lessons about the unseen God*, Welwyn Commentaries (Darlington: Evangelical Press), p. 25.

2 http://www.publications.doh.gov.uk/public/sb0320.htm

The fall of Vashti

Esther 1:12–22

[12]But when the attendants delivered the king's command, Queen Vashti refused to come. Then the king became furious and burned with anger.

[13]Since it was customary for the king to consult experts in matters of law and justice, he spoke with the wise men who understood the times [14]and were closest to the king—Carshena, Shethar, Admatha, Tarshish, Meres, Marsena and Memucan, the seven nobles of Persia and Media who had special access to the king and were highest in the kingdom.

[15]'According to law, what must be done to Queen Vashti?' he asked. 'She has not obeyed the command of King Xerxes that the eunuchs have taken to her.'

[16]Then Memucan replied in the presence of the king and the nobles, "Queen Vashti has done wrong, not only against the king but also against all the nobles and the peoples of all the provinces of King Xerxes. [17]For the queen's conduct will become known to all the women, and so they will despise their husbands and say, 'King Xerxes commanded Queen Vashti to be brought before him, but she would not come.' [18]This very day the Persian and Median women of the nobility who have heard about the queen's conduct will respond to all the king's nobles in the same way. There will be no end of disrespect and discord.

[19]'Therefore, if it pleases the king, let him issue a royal decree and let it be written in the laws of Persia and Media, which cannot be repealed, that Vashti is never again to enter the presence of King Xerxes. Also let the king give her royal position to someone else who is better than she. [20]Then when the king's edict is proclaimed throughout all his vast realm, all the women will respect their husbands, from the least to the greatest.'

[21]The king and his nobles were pleased with this advice, so the king did as Memucan proposed. [22]He sent dispatches to all parts of the kingdom, to each province in its own script and to each people in its own language, proclaiming in each people's tongue that every man should be ruler over his own household.

Chapter 2

The queen's refusal 1:12

When the Lord sent his prophet Samuel to anoint a king over Israel from the sons of Jesse (1 Sam 16), their father naturally enough presented them in order of age and prominence. David, the son whom God had chosen, was not even present. Samuel himself was blind to the souls of the men who stood before him and had to be instructed by the Lord in these words: 'But the Lord said to Samuel, "Do not consider his appearance or his height, for I have rejected him. The Lord does not look at the things man looks at. Man looks at the outward appearance, but the Lord looks at the heart"' (1 Sam. 16:7).

If we have sufficient facts at our disposal, we may at best venture to judge men's actions. The wise man will, however, be very slow to judge the motives that spring from another's heart. John in his Gospel sets before us evidences of the divine nature of the Lord Jesus. One such proof is this right and ability to judge the hearts of men. He can accurately discern Nathanael as a man in whom 'there is nothing false' (John 1:47) and know the unspoken questions spinning around Nicodemus' mind (John 3:2–3). At the Last Supper none of the disciples had umasked the dishonesty and treachery of Judas. Their reaction to the earth-shattering news that one of them would betray the Saviour is not to nudge one another and cast furtive glances towards Judas but to urge the beloved disciple to 'ask him which one he means' (John 13:22–24).

Vashti could have been motivated by any of the following: anger, pride, disdain, dignity, modesty, marital fidelity, love, royal decorum or early feminism. Any of these motives, or a heady cocktail of them all, could have prompted her refusal. One thing is certain—refuse she did, and in doing so she set in motion an epoch-making train of events.

Was she right or wrong? Should she have obeyed her husband and her king?

Submission of a wife to her husband is clearly taught throughout the Scriptures, not merely in well-known proof texts like Ephesians 5:22–24: 'Wives, submit to your husbands as to the Lord. For the husband is the head of the wife as Christ is the head of the church, his body, of which he is the Saviour. Now as the church submits to Christ, so also wives should submit to their husbands in everything.' Wifely submission is integral to the divine order of things from Genesis 1 onwards. There are an abundant number of stories illustrating the maxim of Proverbs 12:4—'A wife of noble character is her husband's crown, but a disgraceful wife is like decay in his bones.' Contrast Abigail (1 Sam. 25) to Jezebel (1 Kings 21). Abigail, married to a stupid, brutish man, seeks to mitigate his worst excesses. Jezebel, married to a weak and greedy man, excels him in evil.

Christians have an equally clear duty to obey those whom God has set over us including the state, as the following scriptures make clear:

Everyone must submit himself to the governing authorities, for there is no authority except that which God has established. The authorities that exist have been established by God. 2 Consequently, he who rebels against the authority is rebelling against what God has instituted, and those who do so will bring judgement on themselves. For rulers hold no terror for those who do right, but for those who do wrong. Do you want to be free from fear of the one in authority? Then do what is right and he will commend you. For he is God's servant to do you good. But if you do wrong, be afraid, for he does not bear the sword for nothing. He is God's servant, an agent of wrath to bring punishment on the wrongdoer. Therefore, it is necessary to submit to the authorities, not only because of possible punishment but also because of conscience.

Romans 13:1–5

I urge, then, first of all, that requests, prayers, intercession and thanksgiving be made for everyone—for kings and all those in authority, that we may live peaceful and quiet lives in all godliness and holiness.

1 Timothy 2:1–2

That duty of submission is not, however, without limitation. The Hebrew midwives in Exodus 1:17 evaded the evil command of Pharaoh to kill all newborn male children. The result, we are told, is that God 'was kind' to them. The command was contrary to the will and law of God so the duty of submission was negated. The exact same reasoning lies behind the answer of Peter and John to the Jewish Sanhedrin when instructed by the latter to cease preaching in the name of Christ: 'Then they called them in again and commanded them not to speak or teach at all in the name of Jesus. But Peter and John replied, "Judge for yourselves whether it is right in God's sight to obey you rather than God. For we cannot help speaking about what we have seen and heard"' (Act 4:18–20).

We may safely conclude that, whatever her motive, Queen Vashti's action was the right one. She set a good example for all women by setting her modesty above the conflicting goal of career advancement. Such principled action is never without consequence. There is no guarantee that we will not be called upon to suffer for doing that which is right. Preserving her dignity cost Vashti her crown.

The king's anger 1:12

As we have noted, an excess of alcohol can rob a man of judgement. We now see that it precipitates hasty actions that are later bitterly regretted. Sinful men typically greet the principled actions of others with anger. The godly are, after all, casting a spotlight on the sin of the ungodly simply by acting in the way they do. Shakespeare quipped that 'Hell has no fury like a woman scorned'; it might be more accurate to reword it 'Hell has no fury like a sinner exposed'. How do we react when others expose our wrongdoing? David, despite his very many failings, is given the accolade a 'man after the Lord's own heart' (1 Sam. 13:14). In 2 Samuel 11–12, David commits a series of terrible sins. He begins with idleness and progresses through lust and adultery to conspiracy and murder. Odd evidence of his godliness, you might think. You would of course be right. It is not until Nathan the Prophet has accused him to his face that his godliness comes to the fore. How will he react? Will he imprison or even kill Nathan? Will he add yet more lies to cover his guilt? Will he rant and rave and proclaim his rights as king? Will he justify himself by turning on the man of God and reminding him that 'none of us is perfect'? Any or all of these would be a common reaction. How did King David react? Scripture records a heartfelt confession followed by praise of the amazing grace and mercy of God.

'Then David said to Nathan, "I have sinned against the LORD." Nathan replied, "The LORD has taken away your sin. You are not going to die"' (2 Sam. 12:13). In this sad story we see the perfect example of the core Christian teaching set out by the Apostle John: 'If we confess our sins, he is faithful and just and will forgive us our sins and purify us from all unrighteousness' (1 John 1:9). Wuest comments on this verse:

The word 'confess' is *homologeō*, from *homos,* 'the same', and *legō,* 'to say', thus, 'to say the same thing as another', or, 'to agree with another'. Confession of sin on the part of the saint means therefore to say the same thing that God does about that sin, to agree with God as to all the implication of that sin as it relates to the Christian who commits it and to a holy God against whom it is committed. [1]

The mark of the child of God is not that he or she does not sin; it lies rather in his or her reaction when God reveals that sin. Xerxes was no child of God. We are told that he 'burned with anger'. Put simply, he completely lost his temper. His rage blinded him to his own foolishness and his love for Vashti. All he was aware of was his humiliation in front of his guests. Vashti had rained on his parade.

A crisis cabinet meeting 1:13–15

It is usually a wise thing to take counsel of others. 'For lack of guidance a nation falls, but many advisers make victory sure' (Prov. 11:14). Kings and powerful men however face particular difficulties in this regard. Counsellors may be afraid to speak with honesty and candour; it takes great courage to say to a leader, 'You are wrong.' The Apostle Paul found himself in such a situation in Antioch (Gal. 2:11–21). The church there had enjoyed great harmony; Jewish and Gentile believers lived and worshipped together without distinction or division. Then one day certain Jews from Jerusalem arrived and things slowly changed; their doctrine and practice began to create discord. They expressed doubts about the propriety of 'eating with Gentile believers'. As a result, Peter and later even Barnabas withdrew their fellowship. Paul grasped that a great gospel issue was at stake; if Gentiles had to become de-facto Jews in order to be truly Christian, then salvation was neither by faith alone nor in Christ alone. Peter was wrong, and Paul was courageous enough to confront him. Sadly in many churches the leadership is regularly and uncharitably taken to task on anything and everything, while in others destructive doctrine and practice goes unchallenged. The people of God should always treat leaders with the respect and honour their office deserves. They must also be ready to challenge wrong teaching and behaviour with humility. Xerxes was not only surrounded by men-pleasers but by people whose primary concern was their own needs and comforts.

Save our civilisation 1:16–18

A shock wave rolled through the gathering. The queen had refused her lord and master. A wife had said no to her husband. A dangerous precedent had been set. Their world of privilege and power was threatened from the very top. Their fear led to a complete over-reaction. Already they saw chaos looming. They were very conscious that Vashti was hosting a parallel banquet at which their own wives would have been present [1:9]. No doubt those wives would have heard both the king's command and the queen's refusal. Were they even now waiting open-mouthed to see what would happen next? Were they already thinking, 'If the queen can do it so can I'? The conclusion drawn by the king's advisors is clear: unless something is done, something firm and decisive, chaos will ensue. 'There will be no end of disrespect and discord' [1:18].

While they were probably guilty of being unduly pessimistic about the outcome of the day's events, their fears were not utterly groundless. There is a very real issue here of example and influence. Every society has role models for good or evil. The choice of our heroes has a profound effect on the shaping of our society. What values do they represent? What pattern do they set for others to follow? The Bible recognises the power of imitation and regulates it wisely. 'Be imitators of God, therefore, as dearly loved children' (Eph. 5:1). 'Remember your leaders, who spoke the word of God to you. Consider the outcome of their way of life and imitate their faith' (Heb. 13:7). 'We do not want you to become lazy, but to imitate those who through faith and patience inherit what has been promised' (Heb. 6:12). 'Dear friend, do not imitate what is evil but what is good. Anyone who does what is good is from God. Anyone who does what is evil has not seen God' (3 John 11).

We have lessons to learn on both sides of this coin. We are all at various time imitators and imitated. We occupy many roles in life where we set examples as parents or grandparents, pastors or teachers, deacons or children's workers, employers or older siblings. All these roles project influence and carry responsibility. We may all want to reflect on Xerxes' behaviour. Is there even the remotest danger that our attitude to alcohol could lead to behaviour we would not want others to copy? Better then, to set aside our liberty and never drink again. This is the conclusion Paul comes to as he reflects on the vexed issue of meat offered to idols. 'Therefore, if what I eat causes my brother to fall into sin, I will never eat meat again, so that I will not cause him to fall' (1 Cor. 8:13). Am I prone to hasty decisions and subject to fits of temper? Then these must be a matter of serious prayer and earnest seeking after God. We must take seriously the command of God: 'Get rid of all bitterness, rage and anger, brawling and slander, along with every form of malice. Be kind and compassionate to one another, forgiving each other, just as in Christ God forgave you' (Eph. 4:31–32).

A victim of self-interest 1:19–22

God alone is omnipotent. Even kings, the most powerful of men, do not have absolute authority. The kings of Persia were not wise enough to leave themselves a 'get-out clause'. The laws of the Medes and Persians were irrevocable. We will see in later chapters how this forms a significant part of the problem God's people face. There is much wisdom in the age-old advice to 'sleep on it'. Major decisions made in the heat of the moment are often regretted in the cool light of day. Xerxes' advisors had their own interests much more to heart than his. It was their domestic superiority rather than his future happiness that dictated their advice. They laid their groundwork well by ensuring that the king's decision was made by royal edict. This left no possibility that the king would later regret and repeal his order of banishment. Once issued such a decree was permanent. Such an arrangement in human affairs is fraught with danger. What if new unforeseen circumstances arose? What if fresh and wiser counsel were to prevail? In the empire of the Medes and the Persians that was simply unfortunate. Once passed such a decree could never be revoked. The king and queen would never see each other again. But no matter: the important thing, as far as the king's advisors were concerned was that 'every man should be ruler over his own household' [1:22]. The crisis was over, the king had been manipulated and the position of his advisors not only preserved but strengthened. Every wife in the empire would now think twice before crossing her lord and master. Act one of the drama has come to a close.

Binding agreements

The issue of binding laws raises many questions. We would probably rejoice if our society held agreements in certain areas as more binding.

Chapter 2

Take marriage. Some marriages tragically end after enormous effort by one partner. Patience and forgiveness, longsuffering love and endurance all fail to rescue the marriage. Sadly, others enter into what was once seen as a binding contract on an almost casual basis and leave it for greener pastures at the slightest provocation.

The Lord takes the matter of oaths and agreements seriously; he expects us to keep the vows we have made before him: 'When you make a vow to God, do not delay in fulfilling it. He has no pleasure in fools; fulfil your vow. It is better not to vow than to make a vow and not fulfil it' (Eccles. 5:4–5). We need to take special notice of those places in Scripture where God himself is said to have sworn an oath. It was with such an oath that he confirmed the permanent nature of Christ's office as our High Priest (Ps. 110:4, Heb. 7:21). We have his sworn word that one day all the nations will bow before him, acknowledging him as their Lord (Isa. 45:23). We may well doubt the wisdom of a weak and foolish man like Xerxes speaking in such binding terms, but not so with God. His wisdom is perfect, his knowledge complete and his word certain.

Reflection/discussion topics from Chapter 2

1 James has a lot of practical advice on judging by outward appearances. *Read* James 2:1–12. Examine your own life and your church in its light. Are all visitors greeted with the same enthusiasm or are we influenced by the car they arrive in and the clothes they wear?

2 *Consider* the role of men and women in the family, the church and the workplace. Are our attitudes determined by the teaching of Scripture, the pressures of contemporary society or self-interest?

3 What would showing love to a wife as Christ loved the church mean in everyday living?

4 When are we as Christians free to disobey lawful authority?

5 What steps can we take to ensure that we do not make hasty decisions or fall prey to bad advice? *Consider* 1 Kings 12; Prov. 12:5,15, 19:20.

6 As Christians we are likely to make 'vows' on a number of occasions: marriage, baptism and church membership for instance. Make a list of those occasions in your own life. What were those vows? What steps are you taking to ensure that you keep them?

Notes

1 **Kenneth S. Wuest,** *Wuest's Word Studies from the Greek New Testament: For the English Reader* (1 Jn 1:9) (Grand Rapids, MI: Eerdmans, 1997).

The search for a queen

Esther 2:1–18

ESTHER MADE QUEEN

1 Later when the anger of King Xerxes had subsided, he remembered Vashti and what she had done and what he had decreed about her. 2 Then the king's personal attendants proposed, 'Let a search be made for beautiful young virgins for the king. 3 Let the king appoint commissioners in every province of his realm to bring all these beautiful girls into the harem at the citadel of Susa. Let them be placed under the care of Hegai, the king's eunuch, who is in charge of the women; and let beauty treatments be given to them. 4 Then let the girl who pleases the king be queen instead of Vashti.' This advice appealed to the king, and he followed it.

5 Now there was in the citadel of Susa a Jew of the tribe of Benjamin, named Mordecai son of Jair, the son of Shimei, the son of Kish, 6 who had been carried into exile from Jerusalem by Nebuchadnezzar king of Babylon, among those taken captive with Jehoiachin king of Judah. 7 Mordecai had a cousin named Hadassah, whom he had brought up because she had neither father nor mother. This girl, who was also known as Esther, was lovely in form and features, and Mordecai had taken her as his own daughter when her father and mother died.

8 When the king's order and edict had been proclaimed, many girls were brought to the citadel of Susa and put under the care of Hegai. Esther also was taken to the king's palace and entrusted to Hegai, who had charge of the harem. 9 The girl pleased him and won his favour. Immediately he provided her with her beauty treatments and special food. He assigned to her seven maids selected from the king's palace and moved her and her maids into the best place in the harem.

10 Esther had not revealed her nationality and family background, because Mordecai had forbidden her to do so. 11 Every day he walked to and fro near the courtyard of the harem to find out how Esther was and what was happening to her.

12 Before a girl's turn came to go in to King Xerxes, she had to complete twelve months

of beauty treatments prescribed for the women, six months with oil of myrrh and six with perfumes and cosmetics. [13] And this is how she would go to the king: Anything she wanted was given to her to take with her from the harem to the king's palace. [14] In the evening she would go there and in the morning return to another part of the harem to the care of Shaashgaz, the king's eunuch who was in charge of the concubines. She would not return to the king unless he was pleased with her and summoned her by name.

[15] When the turn came for Esther (the girl Mordecai had adopted, the daughter of his uncle Abihail) to go to the king, she asked for nothing other than what Hegai, the king's eunuch who was in charge of the harem, suggested. And Esther won the favour of everyone who saw her. [16] She was taken to King Xerxes in the royal residence in the tenth month, the month of Tebeth, in the seventh year of his reign.

[17] Now the king was attracted to Esther more than to any of the other women, and she won his favour and approval more than any of the other virgins. So he set a royal crown on her head and made her queen instead of Vashti. [18] And the king gave a great banquet, Esther's banquet, for all his nobles and officials. He proclaimed a holiday throughout the provinces and distributed gifts with royal liberality.

Second thoughts 2:1

Among the most poignant expressions in the English language is the statement 'he remembered'. A world of sorrow can be conveyed by that simple expression. The exiles in Babylon were reduced to tears when they remembered their homeland: 'By the rivers of Babylon we sat and wept when we remembered Zion' (Ps. 137:1). Their persistent sin and stubborn refusal to heed the warnings of God, through the prophets, had reduced them to servitude in a strange land. As they thought back on their beloved land, they gave way to profound sorrow.

Stripped of his former self-confidence (John 13:37), a heartbroken Peter remembers his former boast that he would die for his Saviour. He remembers his fear at the words of a servant girl identifying him as one of Christ's disciples. He remembers his cowardly betrayal and he weeps (Matt. 26:69–75).

Often the Lord uses such times to draw his people back to himself:

'Whenever God slew them, they would seek him; they eagerly turned to him again. They remembered that God was their Rock, that God Most High was their Redeemer' (Ps. 78:34–35). What Xerxes was experiencing was far more an awareness of his own stupidity and a regret that Vashti was now lost to him for ever.

A brilliant idea 2:2–4

Mumucan and the others knew that it was imperative that the king be lifted out of this melancholy frame of mind. He might be unable to restore the queen, but nothing would stop him taking out his fury on those that had advised him if his happiness was not swiftly restored. Their solution was well suited to his sinful disposition. They proposed an empire-wide beauty contest, and he would get the prize. The finest, purest and fairest would be his to choose from. A new queen would be found, one to satisfy his every desire. The ploy worked and the search was on.

Enter Esther 2:5–8

Now two more of the central characters are introduced: Mordecai and his niece Esther. Consider how God prepared the way for his people. It was Kish the great-grandfather of Mordecai, who was the first of their family to be taken into exile in 597 BC, over a hundred years before Xerxes succeeded to the throne. In the providence of God, Mordecai had settled near the royal court at Susa. He adopted Hadassah, his orphan niece, whom God had endowed with exquisite beauty.

Echoes of Daniel 2:9

How the search for the girls was conducted we are not told, but eventually the choice was made and the young women entered the king's harem. This was an area of the palace reserved for the wives and concubines of the king. It was a society all of its own. The sad epitaph to King Solomon's reign includes this comment: 'He had seven hundred wives of royal birth and three hundred concubines, and his wives led him astray' (1 Kings 11:3).

Once a girl entered that world she could never leave. Marriages were made for a variety of reasons: political alliance, favoured family connections and sometimes even love. In such a world wives could be completely forgotten. What emotions stirred in Esther's heart as she prepared for her future? One thing is certain: she could never have imagined that it was part of a divine purpose that would immortalise her name.

The girls were put into the charge of Hegai. He would have been a eunuch and a man of great influence and power within the harem hierarchy. We again see the hand of God in that, like Joseph (Gen. 39:4, 21) and Daniel (Dan. 1:9) before her, Esther found favour with man because she was in the place of God's choosing.

Typically no expense was spared on either the preparation or the comfort of these potential queens. Already Esther was given a pre-eminence, granted her own servants and elevated to the best part of the harem. Her humility is shown by her willingness to take advice and counsel and receive help from the most unlikely of sources. Hegai was a Gentile and a eunuch; she was a Jewess, yet she had the wisdom to learn from him and so prosper her cause.

How often in the pages of Scripture God's people find themselves, through no fault of their own, in difficult and compromising situations!

Esther's secret 2:10–11

We need to note one other significant fact—her identity had been kept a secret. Her Hebrew name had been changed to a Persian one and her relationship to Mordecai hidden. We are not given the reason for this caution but probably need look no further than the antipathy so often felt by host nations to an immigrant population let alone a captive one. It was certainly once again a decision made under the guiding providence of God. Throughout her lengthy time of preparation, Mordecai kept a watchful eye on her progress and well-being.

Esther the queen 2:12–18

Some four years passed between the deposing of Vashti and the night of Esther's arrival in the presence of the king. This was a once-in-a-lifetime opportunity. Esther had only this one night to impress the king and win his heart. If the king did not subsequently remember her and request her company, she would never see him again. To our minds the whole matter is distasteful if not down right immoral. There is no pre-existent relationship, no wooing and winning, no love prior to the consummation of this 'marriage'. We must, however, be mindful that their world was not ours. In the history of fallen man the ideal of marriage has suffered great abuse. Solomon's excesses were not isolated. All the Patriarchs, with the notable exception of Isaac, were polygamists and recourse to prostitutes was common (Gen. 38, Josh. 6, Judg. 11, 16) though condemned (Prov. 6:26, 23:27). In Esther's world, as in many cultures today, arranged marriages were the norm and her fate no different to that of other girls and perhaps even preferable.

Once again we see the hidden hand of God. The favour Esther gained with Hegai was typical of the effect she had on all who met her. The king would be no exception—God would see to that: 'The king's heart is in the hand of the LORD; he directs it like a watercourse wherever he pleases' (Prov. 21:1). The sovereign Lord saw to it that the heart of the king settled on Esther.

The Hebrew word *aheb*, translated as 'love', has two significant shades of meaning: to have a passion for, and to prefer above.[1] Both are suitable definitions of the effect Esther had on her king. His heart was won and his choice made. Esther was crowned queen and the empire gave a sigh of relief and joined the celebrations.

Chosen

This chapter reminds us again how the Lord brings good out of evil. The selection process for Esther, however refined and perfumed, was in reality a sordid meat market. The women were treated as objects, valued for their looks rather than their godliness. This is the reverse of the Christian ideal set before us in 1 Timothy 2:9–10—'I also want women to dress modestly, with decency and propriety, not with braided hair or gold or pearls or expensive clothes, but with good deeds, appropriate for women who profess to worship God.

The Scriptures speak of another 'choosing' that is of a far different nature. The gracious choice God makes of a people for himself, chosen not because of their beauty, wealth or interest (James 2:5). It is a choosing that takes place in eternity (Eph. 1:11). Those whom God elects receive far more than royal status: 'But you are a chosen people, a royal priesthood, a holy nation, a people belonging to God, that you may declare the praises of him who called you out of darkness into his wonderful light' (1 Peter 2:9).

Reflection/discussion topics from Chapter 3

1 In 1 Corinthians 7:10 Paul contrasts 'godly' and 'worldly' sorrow. The former, he assures us, leaves 'no regret'. Godly sorrow is expressed when we are convicted of our sinful behaviour by the Lord and come to him in repentance and faith. Can you think of examples of both in the Scriptures (e.g. Luke 15:11–32; Heb. 12:16–18)? Can you think of examples in your own experience?

2 Should we ever seek to gain favour with others? Which methods are acceptable in this pursuit and which ones are not? *Consider* the lives of Joseph (Gen. 39–40), Daniel and his friends (Dan. 1–6), and *read* Titus 2:9–10 and 1 Peter 2:18–19.

3 In following Mordecai's advice and concealing her race, is Esther guilty of deceit? Is it ever justifiable to tell lies? If so, under what conditions? *Consider* Exodus 1:15–21 and Joshua 2. How do such histories compare with the principles expressed in Job 27:4 and 1 Peter 2:1–2?

Notes

1 **Archer, Harris and Waltke,** *Theological Wordbook of the Old Testament,* (Chicago: Moody Press, 1980), p14.

The king's life saved

Esther 2:19–23

MORDECAI UNCOVERS A CONSPIRACY

[19]When the virgins were assembled a second time, Mordecai was sitting at the king's gate. [20]But Esther had kept secret her family background and nationality just as Mordecai had told her to do, for she continued to follow Mordecai's instructions as she had done when he was bringing her up.

[21]During the time Mordecai was sitting at the king's gate, Bigthana and Teresh, two of the king's officers who guarded the doorway, became angry and conspired to assassinate King Xerxes. [22]But Mordecai found out about the plot and told Queen Esther, who in turn reported it to the king, giving credit to Mordecai. [23]And when the report was investigated and found to be true, the two officials were hanged on a gallows. All this was recorded in the book of the annals in the presence of the king.

The providence of God 2:19–23

These verses mark a transition in the story and set the scene for the critical events that are to come. Why the virgins were assembled a second time is a mystery; indeed, there is no certainty about their identity. Any girl who had preceded Esther into the king's bedchamber would, from that moment on, be described as a concubine [2:14]. Perhaps these were candidates who might have followed Esther had not the king's heart already been captivated.

Attention is drawn to the change in status experienced by Mordecai. We are now told that he is 'sitting in the gate'. This is a technical phrase and strongly indicates that he now holds an official position at court. Fredric Bush comments:

The phrase might be taken literally, meaning that Mordecai was resorting to the palace area in order to hear further news of Esther's welfare. Most interpreters however understand the phrase in a figurative sense. Since the gate area was the place in the ancient Near East where the legal assembly met (see e.g., Ruth 4) and business was conducted, the 'king's gate' has come to mean 'the royal court in general'. This is made considerably more probable by the discovery of a monumental gate building comprising almost 13,000 square feet and situated some ninety yards east of the palace, unearthed by the French excavations of the 1970s. Wehr has presented evidence from Herodotus and Xenophon as well as Assyrian and Babylonian royal inscriptions that such buildings housed the administrative and supply functions for the royal palace.[1]

In the game of snooker the average amateur is ecstatic when he manages to 'pot' a couple of balls on the trot. A professional, however, is concerned not just with potting the ball in hand, but with positioning the cue ball in such a way that the next two or three shots are 'on'. The Lord has not merely been elevating Esther to the place where she can fulfil her future role. He is ensuring that Mordecai is exactly where he needs to be, precisely when he needs to be there. Men and women are unable to anticipate the next hours with any degree of certainty. What joy and peace floods our hearts when we realise that the Lord has the future in his sovereign control. The hymn writer Joseph Parker has expressed it well:

God holds the key of all unknown,
And I am glad:
If other hands should hold the key,
Or if He trusted it to me,
I might be sad.

What if tomorrow's cares were here
Without its rest?
I'd rather He unlocked the day,
And, as the hours swing open, say
'My will is best.'

The very dimness of my sight
Makes me secure;
For, groping in my misty way,
I feel His hand; I hear Him say,
'My help is sure.'

I cannot read His future plans;
But this I know:
I have the smiling of His face,
And all the refuge of His grace,
While here below.

Enough: this covers all my wants;
And so I rest!
For what I cannot, He can see,
And in His care I saved shall be,
For ever blest.[2]

We are reminded of two other important facts: Esther's nationality is a secret and she is still obedient to her adoptive father despite her newfound status. Scripture often does not burden us with unnecessary detail: such is the case here. We are left in the dark as to what the grievance was that so incensed Bigthana and Teresh. Whatever it was, their anger blinded them to danger. Intrigue and revolt were not unknown in the Persian Empire, but the stakes were very high indeed. To fail in such an endeavour meant certain and painful death. The method of execution was probably impaling the offender after which the body would be hung up as a public warning to others. The narrator does not see fit either to tell us exactly how Mordecai uncovered this plot. This silence contrasts with the great detail later given to the conflict between Mordecai and his implacable enemy Haman. At this point we are simply gathering vital information and marvelling at the wisdom of our God.

Revelation, recording and remembrance 2:21–23

There are clearly good lines of communication all around. Mordecai has no problem in passing on vital information to Esther. She clearly has easy access to the king. She informs the king of the plot, the guilty party and the name of the man to whom he now owes his life.

Persian law swings into action. There should have been three aspects to this:

1 THOROUGH INVESTIGATION OF THE EVIDENCE

It is interesting how even pagan society often prides itself on its system of justice. The king does not simply believe this accusation; he tests it and only when proven does he act. Much later in Bible history the Roman system will be used on more than one occasion to spare the life of the Apostle Paul and ensure that he is able to preach the Gospel in Rome itself (Acts 19:23–41, 22:22–29). God is a God who delights in justice: 'The LORD is known by his justice; the wicked are ensnared by the work of their hands' (Ps. 9:16). 'The LORD works righteousness and justice for all the oppressed' (Ps. 103:6). 'When justice is done, it brings joy to the righteous but terror to evildoers' (Prov. 21:15).

Divine love of justice is of great importance: it sheds light on 1 John 1:9— 'If we confess our sins, he is faithful and just and will forgive us our sins and purify us from all unrighteousness.' We might expect John to tell us that God is 'gracious and merciful' rather than 'just'. Our salvation and security, however, rest on the justice of God as well as on his mercy. When Christ died on the cross he did so as a propitiation for our sins (Rom. 3:25, NKJV). He did so as an atoning sacrifice, and a substitute. He bore the guilt and punishment for all the sins his people had committed and he satisfied the just law of God. The glorious point that John is making is that having once punished Christ for those sins, God could not possibly require us also to be punished. This doctrine is known as 'penal substitutionary atonement', and has historically been at the core of evangelical belief and preaching.

Furthermore, God expects his people to act with justice. The careful balance to be maintained between justice and mercy can be seen in issues of church discipline: 'If your brother sins against you, go and show him his fault, just between the two of you. If he listens to you, you have won your brother over. But if he will not listen, take one or two others along, so that "every matter may be established by the testimony of two or three witnesses". If he refuses to listen to them, tell it to the church; and if he refuses to listen even to the church, treat him as you would a pagan or a tax collector' (Matt. 18:15–17). 'Do not entertain an accusation against an elder unless it is brought by two or three witnesses. Those who sin are to be rebuked publicly, so that the others may take warning' (1 Tim. 5:19–20).

2 PUNISHMENT OF THE GUILTY

Once truth has been established through an investigation of the evidence, justice has two further concerns. Punishing the guilty and vindicating the innocent are both necessary for justice to prevail. God's Law states this as a basic principle: 'Have nothing to do with a false charge and do not put an innocent or honest person to death, for I will not acquit the guilty' (Exod. 23:7). 'When men have a dispute, they are to take it to court and the judges will decide the case, acquitting the innocent and condemning the guilty' (Deut. 25:1). 'Acquitting the guilty and condemning the innocent—the Lord detests them both' (Prov. 17:15).

God's justice should prove a terror to sinners and a comfort to the saved. We often erect a curious double standard in relation to justice. If a judge makes an apparent error in sentencing, the tabloid press is swift to raise a hue and cry. A lenient sentence passed on a paedophile or rapist will result in demands for longer sentences and harsher conditions. On the other hand, if a pensioner is imprisoned for some reason, the demand is for compassion. So far so good. This can be a striving after the ideal set out by Gilbert and Sullivan:

My object all sublime
I shall achieve in time—
To let the punishment fit the crime—
The punishment fit the crime …

The inconsistency occurs when those same people then expect a just God to act unjustly by setting aside the penalty for sin so clearly declared in Scripture: 'The soul who sins is the one who will die' (Ezek. 18:20). 'For the wages of sin is death, but the gift of God is eternal life in Christ Jesus our Lord' (Rom. 6:23). Bigthana and Teresh were guilty of treason and their punishment was death.

3 SUITABLE REWARD FOR THE INNOCENT

When a false accusation was disproved, the innocent party was to be compensated. If an individual uncovered some misdemeanour, then he was suitably rewarded. The unseen hand of God is once more at work. While steps 1 and 2 of the criminal justice system are carried out, step 3 is inexplicably omitted. The king completely overlooks the matter of

Mordecai's reward. This was not only a gross breach of etiquette; it was, in itself, an injustice.

The Persians, like the Medes and Babylonians before them, were great record-keepers. During the time of Ezra, enemies of the Jews sent letters to King Artaxerxes seeking to stop the work on the rebuilding of Jerusalem. Their accusation was that the rebuilding was an act of rebellion not having official sanction. This plan, after initial success, backfired because of Tattenai, governor of Trans-Euphrates, who appealed to the king in these words: 'Now if it pleases the king, let a search be made in the royal archives of Babylon to see if King Cyrus did in fact issue a decree to rebuild this house of God in Jerusalem. Then let the king send us his decision in this matter' (Ezra 5:17).

A search was indeed made—one that vindicated the people of God and ensured their future prosperity and peace. On discovering that the work was being done on the order of Cyrus, Darius (the reigning King at that time) ordered the resumption of the work with the full co-operation of the state and decreed that the expenses incurred be paid from the royal taxes.

In accordance with common practice, a full transcript of the incident was made and Mordecai's deed preserved on record. God had moved yet another piece on the chess board exactly where he wanted it to await the 'end game'.

Reflection/discussion topics from chapter 4

1 How prepared are we to accept our present situation as being part of the great plan of God?

2 Do we spend our time regretting our circumstances or seeking how we may serve God through them?

3 What is the difference between Paul's statement in Philippians 4:11–13 and mere fatalism?

4 Why should the justice of God strike terror into the hearts of sinners?

5 Why does that same justice bring comfort to his people?

6 Are we always just in our dealings with others, or are we sometimes guilty of judging without sufficient evidence?

7 In the matter of church discipline, how can we be careful to weigh all the evidence?

8 What shape should punishing the guilty and vindicating the innocent take in church discipline issues?

9 Justice can seek to be merely punitive, or have an aim of rehabilitation and restoration. Which is appropriate for church discipline? *Consider Galatians 6:1; 1 Corinthians 5:1–13 and the book of Philemon.*

Notes

1 **Fredric Bush,** *Word Biblical Commentary Ruth/Esther* (Word Books, 1996), pp. 372–373.

2 **Joseph Parker,** 1830–1902, *Christian Hymns,* 752.

Haman's hatred

Esther 3:1–6

HAMAN'S PLOT TO DESTROY THE JEWS

3 After these events, King Xerxes honoured Haman son of Hammedatha, the Agagite, elevating him and giving him a seat of honour higher than that of all the other nobles. ²All the royal officials at the king's gate knelt down and paid honour to Haman, for the king had commanded this concerning him. But Mordecai would not kneel down or pay him honour.

³Then the royal officials at the king's gate asked Mordecai, 'Why do you disobey the king's command?' ⁴Day after day they spoke to him but he refused to comply. Therefore they told Haman about it to see whether Mordecai's behaviour would be tolerated, for he had told them he was a Jew.

⁵When Haman saw that Mordecai would not kneel down or pay him honour, he was enraged. ⁶Yet having learned who Mordecai's people were, he scorned the idea of killing only Mordecai. Instead Haman looked for a way to destroy all Mordecai's people, the Jews, throughout the whole kingdom of Xerxes.

Pride fed 3:1–2

Haman is typical of a breed of people we encounter too often in life. He is a small man with far too much authority. Perhaps we first encountered someone like him as a bullying school prefect; we are likely to meet him again in many guises. Often he is little more than an irritation as he seeks to show his importance at others' expense. On occasion he can be a problem of major proportions. He can be found in many walks of life: offices, schools, prisons, even diaconates and elderships.

Xerxes has already demonstrated his lack of judgement. He now acts true to character and elevates petty and mean-minded Haman to a place of pre-eminence, second only to himself. God, in his mercy and for the preservation of his people, has often seen to it that world leaders have godly advisors. He places the latter there to restrain their excesses and direct the paths of the former. Joseph, Daniel and Nehemiah were godly advisors. The sovereign Lord now permits an evil man into such a pre-eminent position. Has God made a mistake, from which he will later have to extricate himself? No! He is demonstrating another principle of his wise governance by showing that:

Therefore once more I will astound these people
with wonder upon wonder;
the wisdom of the wise will perish,
the intelligence of the intelligent will vanish.
 Woe to those who go to great depths
to hide their plans from the LORD,
who do their work in darkness and think,
'Who sees us? Who will know?'

Isaiah 29:14–15

The complexity of God's rule is a delightful subject to dwell upon. He governs nations yet deals justly with individuals. He directs the pathways of men yet never negates their personal moral culpability. He restrains evil but is never its author. We see the complexity of his rule in his dealings with Pharaoh. Scripture asserts both that God hardened Pharaoh's heart and that Pharaoh himself was the author of that hardness (Exod. 7:3, 14:4, 8:15). There is no contradiction here but rather a profound mystery. The Lord governs all things according to his perfect plan, yet leaves men truly the authors of their own actions and justly responsible for the consequences.

Like most small men, Haman loves the adulation of others. He has an overweening pride; he delights in the spectacle of the Persian nobles bowing before him.

Pride dented 3:2–6

If Vashti rained on Xerxes' parade, Mordecai caused it to pour on Haman's. He was a constant irritant because he alone refused to bow and scrape to the newly elevated son of Hammedatha. Mordecai's reasons for this refusal are not made clear. In taking this course of action he was violating a direct command of the king. His reasons must have been compelling for his refusal was not without danger. Two main suggestions have been made.

1 RACIAL

Some have seen great significance in the family tree of these two men. There was an age-old antipathy between the Amalekites and Israel that started in the days of Moses (Exod. 17:16) and was never resolved. Mordecai, a Benjamite, and boasted among his ancestors one 'Kish' [2:5]. Haman is described as an Agagite. These ancestral identifications, despite any difficulties of chronology, draw our attention to the events recorded in 1 Samuel 15. King Saul, the son of Kish, forfeits his kingdom through disobedience to God's command to utterly destroy the Amalekites and King Agag. The suggestion is made that this racial hatred had persisted down the centuries. Now, with descendants of both families thrown together in exile, it surfaces again, with fatal consequences. Some would go further and see redemptive significance. The aim of Haman is nothing short of genocide, the utter destruction of the people of God. If the children of Abraham perish, how can the Messiah, the Son of David, assume his throne and fulfil his ministry? If this is indeed so, then what we have here is nothing less than a major skirmish in a far greater battle—that between the Lamb and the beast spoken of in Revelation 17:12–14—'The ten horns you saw are ten kings who have not yet received a kingdom, but who for one hour will receive authority as kings along with the beast. They have one purpose and will give their power and authority to the beast. They will make war against the Lamb, but the Lamb will overcome them because he is Lord of lords and King of kings—and with him will be his called, chosen and faithful followers.'

2 PERSONAL

If we reject the first explanation, we are left with variations on the second. Was there some personal history between these two men? None is mentioned. Was Mordecai a good judge of character? Did he despise Haman because he knew him to be an evil man? Least likely, was

Mordecai too proud to give the honour due Haman's by right of the king's decree?

On balance, the first suggestion seems to have most merit. It takes into account the fact that the inspired writer cites these historical details, which otherwise seem to have no significance.

Reflection/discussion topics from Chapter 5

1 Pride has been the downfall of many men. *Consider* the biblical examples of Uzziah (2 Chron. 26), Hezekiah (2 Chron. 32:24–33), Nebuchadnezzar (Dan. 4), Herod (Acts 12:19–25). What do we see as the causes of and remedies for such pride?

2 In what ways can pride be manifested in our lives?

3 Is it right for Christians to honour other Christians or even unbelievers? *Consider* Exodus 20:12; Romans 2:8, 12:10, 13:7; Philippians 2:25–30; 1 Timothy 5:17; 1 Peter 2:17.

4 How should we appropriately honour these varied groups of people?

5 There is much evidence of national/racial feuding in the pages of Scripture. *Consider* Galatians 3:26–29; Ephesians 2:11–22 and Revelation 5:9–10. Do these verses warrant our holding antagonism towards someone on the grounds of race or nationality?

Kill the Jews

Esther 3:7–15

7In the twelfth year of King Xerxes, in the first month, the month of Nisan, they cast the *pur* (that is, the lot) in the presence of Haman to select a day and month. And the lot fell on the twelfth month, the month of Adar.

8Then Haman said to King Xerxes, 'There is a certain people dispersed and scattered among the peoples in all the provinces of your kingdom whose customs are different from those of all other people and who do not obey the king's laws; it is not in the king's best interest to tolerate them. 9If it pleases the king, let a decree be issued to destroy them, and I will put ten thousand talents of silver into the royal treasury for the men who carry out this business.'

10So the king took his signet ring from his finger and gave it to Haman son of Hammedatha, the Agagite, the enemy of the Jews. 11'Keep the money,' the king said to Haman, 'and do with the people as you please.'

12Then on the thirteenth day of the first month the royal secretaries were summoned. They wrote out in the script of each province and in the language of each people all Haman's orders to the king's satraps, the governors of the various provinces and the nobles of the various peoples. These were written in the name of King Xerxes himself and sealed with his own ring. 13Dispatches were sent by couriers to all the king's provinces with the order to destroy, kill and annihilate all the Jews—young and old, women and little children—on a single day, the thirteenth day of the twelfth month, the month of Adar, and to plunder their goods. 14A copy of the text of the edict was to be issued as law in every province and made known to the people of every nationality so that they would be ready for that day.

15Spurred on by the king's command, the couriers went out, and the edict was issued in the citadel of Susa. The king and Haman sat down to drink, but the city of Susa was bewildered.

Trusting to luck 3:7

GK Chesterton famously said that 'When people stop believing in God, they don't believe in nothing—they believe in anything.' One great reality of our present, sophisticated, scientific age is its overwhelming superstition. Do your own research by going to your local bookshop and measuring the size of the section covering self-help manuals and New Age literature. A search powered by Google on the worldwide web for the topic 'horoscopes' produced sixty-seven pages of relevant sites to visit. Many people, too rational to believe in God, are happy to believe that their destinies are controlled by the time and place of their birth and the position in space of rock and gas (the planets and the stars). Multi-national firms allow their decision-making processes to be influenced by such thinking. Haman was such a man; he consulted his gods for an auspicious day to set in motion an evil plot.

The casting of lots was known in Israel (Josh. 18:10, 1 Chron. 24–26, Neh. 10–11) as well as the surrounding nations (Ezek. 21, Obad. 11, Jonah 1:7). The last recorded incident in Scripture takes place in Acts 1:26—'Then they cast lots, and the lot fell to Matthias; so he was added to the eleven apostles.' After the betrayal and suicide of Judas the remaining eleven Apostles cast lots to appoint his successor. The man they choose is Matthias. No further mention is ever made of him. The apostle most prominent in the future growth of the church was instead Paul. In Acts 2 the Holy Spirit is poured out on the church and a new era of guidance and direction is born. Future generations of God's people will have no need of 'lots'; they will have an authoritative, inerrant, inspired canon of Scripture and an indwelling Holy Spirit to guide them.

However men seek their guidance, the Lord maintains his gracious control over their affairs: 'The lot is cast into the lap, but its every decision is from the LORD' (Prov. 16:33).

Deceiving the king 3:8–9

Five years have passed since Esther became queen and still her identity is a secret. The time chosen for the genocide is almost a year into the future. Plenty of time for a weak king to be manipulated and an empire bent to the will of an evil man. Deception can often be a subtle mixture of truth, half-truths and outright lies. This is the precise cocktail that Haman brings before the king.

Truth—The Jews are dispersed throughout the empire. Their customs are different from those of the nations among whom they dwell. Theirs are customs fashioned by the laws of their God and shaped by their ethnic history.

Half-truth—There are occasions when they will 'break the law'. Those occasions, however, are always determined by their primary allegiance to their God (Dan. 3, 6). On the whole they are law-abiding, loyal and productive citizens of the king.

Lies—The king's best interests are certainly not served by the destruction of this people. God frequently blesses individuals and nations, simply because of the presence within them, of his people. The household of Potiphar prospered as a direct result of the blessing of God on Joseph (Gen. 39:2–6). The children of İsrael were still looking to the Lord to fulfil the promise made long ago to the first exiles carried away to Babylon:

This is what the Lord Almighty, the God of Israel, says to all those I carried into exile from Jerusalem to Babylon: "Build houses and settle down; plant gardens and eat what they produce. Marry and have sons and daughters; find wives for your sons and give your daughters in marriage, so that they too may have sons and daughters. Increase in number there; do not decrease. Also, seek the peace and prosperity of the city to which I have carried you into exile. Pray to the Lord for it, because if it prospers, you too will prosper.

Jeremiah 29:4–7

Haman provides the perfect illustration of the kind of person God is said to hate: 'There are six things the LORD hates, seven that are detestable to him: haughty eyes, a lying tongue, hands that shed innocent blood, a heart that devises wicked schemes, feet that are quick to rush into evil, a false witness who pours out lies and a man who stirs up dissension among brothers' (Prov. 6:16–19).

Abdicating authority 3:10–11

The depth of Xerxes' callousness is seen in the obscenely casual way in which he acquiesces to Haman's evil plan. A nation is to be eradicated, an entire people's history, culture and very existence is to be snuffed out, yet no enquiry at all is made. Think of all the questions that should have tumbled from Xerxes' lips. What people are these? How do they come to be in my kingdom? What are these strange customs they practise? Which of my laws do they flout? Are they all as guilty as each other? Why has no one told of this danger to my rule before? Yet not one single query passes his lips. He is prepared to sanction genocide on the unsubstantiated word of one man. His suspicions are not even aroused when Haman offers to pay the costs of this patriotic massacre. This is more than naivety, more than callousness: this is unmitigated evil.

Xerxes brushes aside the offer of money and signs away the lives of thousands and thousands of his loyal subjects. We would be wrong to assume that this means that Haman will not still have to pay up, a view supported by the fact that Mordecai later tells Esther the exact sum involved [4:7]. The refusal is 'eastern politeness'; a ready acceptance on the part of the king would seem grasping and undermine his dignity. What we have here is a form of bargaining seen elsewhere in Scripture (Gen. 23, 2 Sam. 24:18–25) and that still goes on to this day. Each party has to be seen to be generous, not mercenary. The reality is that at the end of the day Haman will pay. He no doubt expects to redeem his losses by plundering the Jews on the day of their destruction.

The staggering implications of what was plotted is thrown into sharp relief in the final words of this section: 'The king and Haman sat down to drink, but the city of Susa was bewildered' [15].

Disaster looms 3:12–15

The diabolical nature of the plan is graphically seen in the repeated horror of verse 13—'to destroy, kill and annihilate all the Jews—young and old, women and little children—on a single day'. This is in all probability not just a comment on the decree but a direct quotation from it. Haman seeks to end all ambiguity and close the door on all compassion. No one at all is to be spared; men and women, young and old—all must die and die on one single day. There will be no place on the known earth for them to hide and the order is given by sealed royal edict. It cannot be rescinded, not even by the king.

Swiftly the messengers of doom are dispatched to the ends of the earth so that a people may await their appointed annihilation. The bewilderment felt in Susa may well have been repeated throughout the empire. Some no doubt were pleased at the opportunity to settle old scores, others enticed by the prospect of plundering the wealth of the Jews. The upright would be appalled by such an unwarranted slaughter of innocent people. The wise perhaps wondered who would be next.

Reflection/discussion topics from chapter 6

1 Is it ever right for a Christian to consult a horoscope? *Consider* Jeremiah 2:13 and Deuteronomy 4:15–20.

2 Some people seek their guidance from what they believe to be the spirits of the dead. How does God view such practices? *Consider* Isaiah 8:19; Leviticus 19:31, 20:6, 27 and 1 Samuel 28.

3 The Bible has much to say about truth. How much do you think truthfulness is a distinguishing mark of the Christian? *Consider* Psalms 15:2, 51:6, 86:11, 119:30, 145:48 and 2 Corinthians 4:2.

4 Is the converse also true that without God men are predisposed to lies? *Consider* John 8:44; Psalm 10:2–7; Romans 1:25, 2:8 and 2 Timothy 3:7, 4:4.

5 Xerxes abdicated the authority God had given to him. The pattern for the exercise of authority is to be found in God's rule over his people. What are the characteristics of that rule? *Consider* Psalm 23.

6 God has appointed many roles of authority, in government, family and church. What are they and how should they be exercised?

7 Are any of these roles, which we fulfil? How faithful are we in performing them? *Consider* Romans 13:1–7; *also* Ephesians 5:22–33; Titus 2:3–5; 1 Peter 3:1–7; *also* Colossians 3:21; *also* 1 Peter 5:1–4.

8 Part of the charge against the Jews was that they were different. Does different always mean worse? Is there anything we can learn from the mixture of cultures that make up our modern society?

9 Should Christians be seen as different? If so, in what ways? *Consider* Acts 4:13; Titus 2:12–14 and 2 Peter 3:11–12.

Esther's choice

Esther 4:

MORDECAI PERSUADES ESTHER TO HELP

[1]When Mordecai learned of all that had been done, he tore his clothes, put on sackcloth and ashes, and went out into the city, wailing loudly and bitterly. [2]But he went only as far as the king's gate, because no one clothed in sackcloth was allowed to enter it. [3]In every province to which the edict and order of the king came, there was great mourning among the Jews, with fasting, weeping and wailing. Many lay in sackcloth and ashes.

[4]When Esther's maids and eunuchs came and told her about Mordecai, she was in great distress. She sent clothes for him to put on instead of his sackcloth, but he would not accept them. [5]Then Esther summoned Hathach, one of the king's eunuchs assigned to attend her, and ordered him to find out what was troubling Mordecai and why.

[6]So Hathach went out to Mordecai in the open square of the city in front of the king's gate. [7]Mordecai told him everything that had happened to him, including the exact amount of money Haman had promised to pay into the royal treasury for the destruction of the Jews. [8]He also gave him a copy of the text of the edict for their annihilation, which had been published in Susa, to show to Esther and explain it to her, and he told him to urge her to go into the king's presence to beg for mercy and plead with him for her people.

[9]Hathach went back and reported to Esther what Mordecai had said. [10]Then she instructed him to say to Mordecai, [11]'All the king's officials and the people of the royal provinces know that for any man or woman who approaches the king in the inner court without being summoned the king has but one law: that he be put to death. The only exception to this is for the king to extend the gold sceptre to him and spare his life. But thirty days have passed since I was called to go to the king.'

[12]When Esther's words were reported to Mordecai, [13]he sent back this answer: 'Do not think that because you are in the king's house you alone of all the Jews will escape.

14For if you remain silent at this time, relief and deliverance for the Jews will arise from another place, but you and your father's family will perish. And who knows but that you have come to royal position for such a time as this?'

15Then Esther sent this reply to Mordecai: 16'Go, gather together all the Jews who are in Susa, and fast for me. Do not eat or drink for three days, night or day. I and my maids will fast as you do. When this is done, I will go to the king, even though it is against the law. And if I perish, I perish.'

17So Mordecai went away and carried out all of Esther's instructions.

Weeping and wailing 4:1–3

Though the name of God is not mentioned in the book of Esther, his footprints, as we have seen, are everywhere. The immediate effect of the publishing of the Edict of Destruction is to cause Mordecai to don sackcloth and cover himself with ashes. To our modern western minds this is strange behaviour. It was not so in the ancient near east; it was an everyday occurrence and sent a clear and unmistakable message.

MOURNING

Dressing in sackcloth and ashes was a sign of deep sadness and mourning. When Jacob is deceived into believing that his beloved son Joseph is dead (Gen. 37); this was the outward expression of his bitter grief. Scripture abounds with other such examples (2 Sam. 3:31, Jer. 6:26, Lam. 2:10–11).

REPENTANCE

Scriptural examples show that mourning was closely allied to repentance. When Jonah confronted the Ninevites and God granted them the gift of repentance, they immediately expressed their grief and sorrow in exactly this way. Indeed, the King of Nineveh passed a decree that every man and beast fast and dress in sackcloth. The Lord Jesus chastised the inhabitants of Korazin and Bethsaida by telling them that even the Gentiles of Tyre and Sidon would have repented and worn sackcloth if they had seen the miracles that he had performed among them (Matt. 11:21).

If we are wise, we will also see the clear message of Mordecai's actions. There is of course the natural mourning any man would feel if his own life, the lives of his loved ones, indeed his whole nation, hung in the balance. We should, however, look deeper. When faced with adversity the first reaction of the godly should surely be to enquire whether or not they are the authors of their own destruction. They should humbly seek to discover if the calamity they face is perhaps a just and deserved punishment from God. Isaiah reacts to the vision he has of God in the Temple (Isa. 6) with a realisation of his own and the nation's sinfulness. Jesus seeks to teach his disciples the same lesson from the tragedy involving the tower at Siloam (Luke 13:4–5). His divine counsel is 'examine your own heart'. Often the appearance of angelic visitors among humans produced fear and even despair (Num. 22, Judg. 13, Luke 2), requiring God's specific reassurance to quell them. The more we are aware of God's holiness and our sinfulness, the less we will carp and complain when problems arise. Instead of asking 'why?' we may well start asking 'why not?'

Mordecai would have known that time and again God had chastised his people through their enemies. He may well have wondered if the Persians should be added to the long list that already included Egyptians, Moabites, Philistines, Syrians, Assyrians, Babylonians and many others. God had wisely permitted Israel's slavery in Egypt, their subjugation to heathen nations, and exile. Might he now be purging them again?

FASTING

The same reasoning can safely be applied to the matter of fasting. Just as sorrowful repentance is assumed in the mention of sackcloth and ashes, so prayer is assumed in the practice of fasting. Abstaining from food is merely dieting unless there is some spiritual intent and action. Isaiah made this clear, when, the people of his day complained that their fasting had not had the desired effect on God. The prophet's response was to expose the reality that theirs was not true fasting. It lacked humility and self-denial; it was instead an occasion for conflict and violence. He reminded them that social justice was a pre-requisite of true fasting (Isa. 58). Because fasting is set in the context of 'calling on the Lord', it seems that prayer is assumed. Elsewhere the link between these two practices is made explicit. Ezra, facing the threat of bandits and ashamed to turn to a pagan king for aid, fasts and prays (Ezra 8). Nehemiah, distressed at the reported state of his beloved Jerusalem, fasts and prays (Neh. 1). Daniel, on discovering the prophecies of Jeremiah concerning his own day, fasts and prays for wisdom (Dan. 9). The prophetess Anna, her life lived waiting the coming of her Messiah, spends her days in the Temple in fasting and prayer (Luke 2:36–40). This Old Testament practice is still honoured in New Testament days, so that when Paul and Barnabas are set apart for mission service (Acts 13:3) or elders are appointed in fledgling churches (Acts 14:23), it is with this twin accompaniment. Prayer may not be explicitly mentioned, but it is hardly hidden in the actions of Mordecai.

A queen's concern 4:4–5

Life in the harem was a secluded affair. The wives and concubines of the 'great king' were shielded from anything that might disturb or distress them. This was part of an elaborate attempt to shield the king himself from anything that might cloud his happiness. This practice of seclusion explains the otherwise inexplicable reaction of Nehemiah in Nehemiah 2:1–2—'In the month of Nisan in the twentieth year of King Artaxerxes, when wine was brought for him, I took the wine and gave it to the king. I had not been sad in his presence before; so the king asked me, "Why does your face look so sad when you are not ill? This can be nothing but sadness of heart." I was very much afraid.'

Nehemiah's fear was well grounded. By appearing in the king's presence with anything but a happy smile on his face, he had committed a great transgression of both etiquette and law. The consequences, save for the hand of God, could have been extreme.

Esther and Mordecai had, with the help of the eunuchs and others, established a chain of communication between them that was to prove critical. She soon became aware of Mordecai's distress but remained ignorant of the cause. Her initial reaction was to encourage him to 'cheer up'. Mordecai responded by giving her a full account of the impending disaster. He made sure that she saw a copy of the edict so that no doubt could remain in her mind. Having done this he urged her to intercede with the king on behalf of her people.

Knowledge and responsibility 4:6–9

Knowledge brings with it responsibility. The moment Esther became aware of the need, she became accountable for her actions. This simple truth has profound implications. The proclamation of the gospel increases the culpability of mankind: 'In the past God overlooked such ignorance, but now he commands all people everywhere to repent' (Acts 17:30).

Men are, of course, fully accountable even before hearing the gospel; they have, after all, the witness of creation (Ps. 19:1, Rom. 1:20), the Law and conscience (Rom. 2:12–16). That responsibility is, however, heightened after they have been exposed to full gospel light. Having made known to the Athenians the true name and nature of their unknown god, the Apostle Paul warned them that God therefore commanded them to repent (Acts 17:30).

It has been well said that 'Without knowledge there is no concern, without concern there is no prayer, without prayer there is no action, without action there is no change'. As Christians we have an obligation to be informed in order that we might be prayerful. Part of the commission given to Ezra was to 'enquire about Judah and Jerusalem with regard to the Law of your God' (Ezra 7). Similarly, Nehemiah's ministry begins when he questions Hanani 'about the Jewish remnant that survived the exile, and also about Jerusalem.' When we have knowledge that would benefit others we are obliged to share it. When we are in ignorance we should always seek light.

The cost of discipleship 4:10–11

Some have been swift to condemn Esther for her response to this tragic news. Her reaction, however, is simply human and very understandable. We need to be ever grateful that our heavenly Father is often more compassionate to us than we are to one another: 'As a father has compassion on his children, so the LORD has compassion on those who fear him; for he knows how we are formed, he remembers that we are dust' (Ps. 103:13–14).

Her reply to Mordecai was in effect simply to say, 'Do you have any idea what you are asking?' A month had elapsed since she had been summoned to the king, with whom initiative always rested. Theirs was no partnership of equals. She existed to please her master and he decided when and where to take pleasure of her. To presume to enter the king's presence uninvited produced an automatic sentence of death. This king had struck the crown from one queen's head for failing to come when commanded; he could easily remove the head of another coming unbidden. Esther was being invited to join a very select group of people—those who would lay down their lives for others (see John 15:13).

The person of Christ

Those few who walked this path serve to highlight the remarkable nature of the ministry of the Lord Jesus Christ. Esther was being asked to risk her life for her own deliverance and that of her family and nation. The Lord commends his love in a far more remarkable way: 'But God demonstrates his own love for us in this: While we were still sinners, Christ died for us' (Rom. 5:8). The old hymn expresses it well:

Thou didst leave Thy throne
And Thy kingly crown,
When Thou camest to earth for me; ...
Heaven's arches rang
When the angels sang,
Proclaiming Thy royal degree;
But of lowly birth
Cam'st Thou, Lord, on earth,
And in great humility:
O come to my heart, Lord Jesus!
There is room in my heart for Thee.[1]

Christ exchanged all the glory of heaven to seek and save rebel sinners. He faced not the possibility of death but its certainty. The suffering he willingly undertook is prophetically described in Psalm 22. The depth of that suffering is heard in his cry of dereliction on the cross: 'From the sixth hour until the ninth hour darkness came over all the land. About the ninth hour Jesus cried out in a loud voice, "Eloi, Eloi, lama sabachthani?"—which means, "My God, my God, why have you forsaken me?"' (Matt. 27:45–46).

Its purpose was revealed in the words of the Apostle Peter: 'For Christ died for sins once for all, the righteous for the unrighteous, to bring you to God. He was put to death in the body but made alive by the Spirit' (1 Peter

3:18). And again, 'He himself bore our sins in his body on the tree, so that we might die to sins and live for righteousness; by his wounds you have been healed' (1 Peter 2:24). To plumb the unfathomable depths of that willing sacrifice for sinners is the constant quest of the Christian:

Give me a sight, O Saviour,
Of Thy wondrous love to me,
Of the love that brought Thee down to earth,
To die on Calvary.

O make me understand it,
Help me to take it in,
What it meant to Thee, the Holy One,
To bear away my sin.

Was it the nails O Saviour,
That bound Thee to the tree?
Nay, 'twas Thine everlasting love,
Thy love for me, for me.

O wonder of all wonders,
That through Thy death for me
My open sins, my secret sins,
Can all forgiven be!

Then melt my heart, O Saviour,
Bend me, yes, break me down,
Until I own Thee Conqueror,
And Lord and Sovereign crown.

Katharine Agnes May Kelly[2]

Trust or perish 4:12–14

If at first glance Esther's message seems cowardly, so Mordecai's response may seem harsh. There are times, however, when we need to 'tell it as it is'; this was such an occasion. Some things are too important to permit any ambiguity. The Psalmist sees salvation in this light: 'I do not hide your righteousness in my heart; I speak of your faithfulness and salvation. I do not conceal your love and your truth from the great assembly' (Ps. 40:10). God in his gracious self-disclosure does the same: 'I have not spoken in secret, from somewhere in a land of darkness; I have not said to Jacob's descendants, "Seek me in vain." I, the Lord, speak the truth; I declare what is right' (Isa. 45:19). Hence the prayer of the persecuted disciples is: 'Now, Lord, consider their threats and enable your servants to speak your word with great boldness' (Acts 4:29).

It is imperative that Esther be in no doubt concerning her plight. She will perish along with her people. The remarkable faith of Mordecai is seen in that his trust is not in Esther's position of influence but in the sovereign God. He fully understands that she is only an instrument in the Lord's hand. It is the hand, not the instrument that will deliver. If Esther is disobedient, she will suffer personal consequences but the gracious purposes of God will in no way be frustrated. 'To the angel of the church in Philadelphia write: "These are the words of him who is holy and true, who holds the key of David. What he opens no one can shut, and what he shuts no one can open"' (Rev. 3:7). We are never indispensable in God's plan, but we are always responsible for our obedience to it.

Remember Joseph 4:14

When Joseph finally revealed himself to his shocked and fearful brothers, he displayed the depth of his faith:

Then Joseph said to his brothers, 'Come close to me.' When they had done so, he said, 'I am your brother Joseph, the one you sold into Egypt! And now, do not be distressed and do not be angry with yourselves for selling me here, because it was to save lives that God sent me ahead of you. For two years now there has been famine in the land, and for the next five years there will not be ploughing and reaping. But God sent me ahead of you to preserve for you a remnant on earth and to save your lives by a great deliverance.

So then, it was not you who sent me here, but God. He made me father to Pharaoh, lord of his entire household and ruler of all Egypt.

Genesis 45:4–8

He asserts that it was not by accident that he was where and who he was at that moment. Neither was it merely the result of his brothers' treachery. He has full confidence to say 'it was not you who sent me here, but God'.

Mordecai urges Esther to see beyond the outward events and discern a possible plan of God. Hindsight is never possible until everything has worked itself out. Providence is often only discernible when God's plan is completed. This is why Paul reminds the Corinthian Christians that 'We live by faith, not by sight' (2 Cor. 5:7). In the letter to the Romans he expresses it thus: ' And we know that in all things God works for the good of those who love him, who have been called according to his purpose' (Rom. 8:28). It is not always given to us, however, to know exactly how that applies to a given situation at a precise moment.

Stand with me 4:15–17

Esther is wise enough and humble enough to know that this great venture will prosper only if it is indeed the will of God. She therefore embarks on a course that displays considerable wisdom. She herself is to fast (and pray). She has evidently surrounded herself with godly maidservants who will join her in this venture. She now begs Mordecai to gather all the Jews in Susa. Together this great company will seek God without respite for three days and nights.

Crises require extraordinary measures. Prayer should be part of the fabric of every Christian's life. One of the shortest verses in our English Bible is 1 Thessalonians 5:17 which simply urges us to 'pray continually'. Following his general exhortation to pray, Paul urges the Ephesian Christians to constant prayer and intercession: 'Take the helmet of salvation and the sword of the Spirit, which is the word of God. And pray in the Spirit on all occasions with all kinds of prayers and requests. With this in mind, be alert and always keep on praying for all the saints' (Eph. 6:17–18). Paul immediately adds a personal plea, ' Pray also for me, that whenever I open my mouth, words may be given me so that I will fearlessly make known the mystery of the gospel' (Eph. 6:19).

SPECIAL PRAYER

The Gospels record that before Jesus chose his disciples, he spent the night in solitary prayer (Luke 6:12–14). It was again in prayer that he spent the hours before his arrest, seeking on that occasion the fellowship of his inner group of disciples (Matt. 26:36–46). When the Apostle Peter was imprisoned, the infant church gathered together for urgent prayer (Acts 12:1–19). Throughout its history the church of God has gathered together in times of special need and sought the mercy of God. They have cried out to him with the urgency and confidence of the Psalmist:

Hear, O Lord, and answer me,
for I am poor and needy.
Guard my life, for I am devoted to you.
You are my God; save your servant
who trusts in you.
Have mercy on me, O Lord,
for I call to you all day long.
Bring joy to your servant,
for to you, O Lord,
I lift up my soul.
You are forgiving and good, O Lord,
abounding in love to all who call to you.
Hear my prayer, O Lord;
listen to my cry for mercy.
In the day of my trouble I will call to you,
for you will answer me.
Among the gods there is none like you, O Lord;
no deeds can compare with yours.

Psalm 86:1–8

PERSONAL PRAYER

Great servants of God have never been above seeking prayer for themselves. If, as we have seen, even Jesus requested the fellowship of his disciples in prayer (Matt. 26:38), and Paul makes a similar request of the Ephesians (Eph. 6:19), how much more do we stand in that need! Esther knew the magnitude of the task before her and dared not embark on it without the prayers of God's people.

The wicked sometimes show sense in this regard. Hard-hearted Pharaoh begged Moses for his prayers (Exod. 8:8–9), as did Jeroboam with the unnamed 'man of God' (1 Kings 13). We all need the prayers of other Christians. How foolish if we allow pride to prevent us from asking for them! Hugh Stowell puts it this way in his hymn 'From every stormy wind that blows':

There is a spot where spirits blend,
Where friend holds fellowship with friend;
Though sundered far, by faith we meet
Around one common mercy-seat.[3]

Into the furnace 4:17

The final words of Esther in this chapter are full of faith and humble submission: 'And if I perish, I perish' [4:16]. In every crisis our trust in God must go beyond care for our personal safety and well-being. We must commit to doing what is right simply because it is right, whatever the possible outcome. A similar commitment is recorded in Daniel 3. King Nebuchadnezzar has had a gigantic idol erected in the plain of Dura and commanded all his subjects to bow down and worship it. Shadrach, Meshach and Abednego, however, served not man but the true God and refused. Threatened with being cast into a fiery furnace their response was:

Shadrach, Meshach and Abednego replied to the king, 'O Nebuchadnezzar, we do not need to defend ourselves before you in this matter. If we are thrown into the blazing furnace, the God we serve is able to save us from it, and he will rescue us from your hand, O king. But even if he does not, we want you to know, O king, that we will not serve your gods or worship the image of gold you have set up.'

Daniel 3:16–18

That same spirit is now seen in Esther. Her fate rests in the hands of God. She does not know what will befall her, but she like them will not bow the knee. In the early years of mission work in Africa, life expectancy was measured in weeks and months rather than in years. Many pioneers buried their husband or wife and children rather than deny their missionary calling. If the spirit that was in Esther is to be found in us, each generation needs to reflect on such heroes of the faith as John and Betty Stam, and Jim Elliot. We need to be aware of the cost the churches in such places as Korea and Cambodia have paid that Christ might be made known.

Reflection/discussion topics from Chapter 7

1 What part do you think fasting should play in the life of individual Christians and churches today?

2 How could we ensure that it does not simply become a meaningless external ritual?

3 Does repentance have any part to play in the life of a Christian after conversion?

4 *Consider* 2 Corinthians 7:8–13, 12:20–21 and Revelation 2–3.

5 If we have a responsibility to become aware of the needs of individuals, the church, and the wider world, how can we acquire such knowledge?

6 Do we read newsletters and magazines from; the mission field and Christian organisations involved in social and ethical issues?

7 How willing are we to 'suffer' for the sake of the gospel?

8 Can we shed light on the real answer to Question 6 by looking at our gifts of time and money and our involvement in Christian work?

9 How aware are we of the suffering church in our own day?

Notes

1 **Emily Elizabeth Steele Elliott,** 1836–97, *Christian Hymns,* 183.
2 **Katharine Agnes May Kelly,** 1869–1942, *Christian Hymns,* 205.
3 **Hugh Stowell,** 1799–1865, *Christian Hymns,* 382.

Approaching the king

Esther 5:1–8

ESTHER'S REQUEST TO THE KING

[1]On the third day Esther put on her royal robes and stood in the inner court of the palace, in front of the king's hall. The king was sitting on his royal throne in the hall, facing the entrance. [2]When he saw Queen Esther standing in the court, he was pleased with her and held out to her the gold sceptre that was in his hand. So Esther approached and touched the tip of the sceptre.

[3]Then the king asked, 'What is it, Queen Esther? What is your request? Even up to half the kingdom, it will be given you.'

[4]'If it pleases the king,' replied Esther, 'let the king, together with Haman, come today to a banquet I have prepared for him.'

[5]'Bring Haman at once,' the king said, 'so that we may do what Esther asks.'

So the king and Haman went to the banquet Esther had prepared. [6]As they were drinking wine, the king again asked Esther, 'Now what is your petition? It will be given you. And what is your request? Even up to half the kingdom, it will be granted.'

[7]Esther replied, 'My petition and my request is this: [8]If the king regards me with favour and if it pleases the king to grant my petition and fulfil my request, let the king and Haman come tomorrow to the banquet I will prepare for them. Then I will answer the king's question.'

Appropriately dressed 5:1

There are few better examples than the one we find here of the wise advice given in Matthew 10:16—'I am sending you out like sheep among wolves. Therefore be as shrewd as snakes and as innocent as doves.'

We have seen that Esther resigned herself to whatever future God had planned for her. She was prepared even to die in his service. There is no incompatibility between this resolve and her cautious wisdom. Esther makes every effort to avoid conflict with the king; she makes herself as attractive as she can by dressing in her finest royal robes. She then positions herself demurely. The place she chose to stand was strategic. She was near enough that the king could not fail to see her yet discreet enough for it not to be a too obvious violation of protocol.

The sceptre extended 5:2

Her venture was still extremely hazardous. If he saw her at a moment of anger or irritation she would be undone. The king would not need to condemn her. Condemnation was assumed, with the sentence already prescribed—the penalty was death. Her only hope lay in the king's intervention. The moment her presence was detected, the guard would be alert and every eye turned towards the king. To secure her death, he simply need turn his eyes away and she would be swept from his presence to her execution. Mercy was his prerogative alone. Only he could spare her and indicate his acceptance of her intrusion by extending the 'golden sceptre', the emblem of his authority. (We will consider the remarkable picture of Christ contained here at the end of the chapter.) The sovereign God melted the king's heart and Esther was not merely spared but warmly welcomed.

Half my kingdom 5:3

An empty extravagance is seen in his sweeping promise that he will grant any request, even half his kingdom. Our actions are determined by our hearts, and similar offers or opportunities expose what lies within them. Esther is seeking the life of her people. Mark in his Gospel (Mark 6:14–29) records another incident when a king makes an identical offer. The king was Herod, the occasion a drunken revel in which both monarch and guests had been aroused by the dancing of his stepdaughter. Delighted with her entertainment, Herod makes his foolish boast: 'When the daughter of Herodias came in and danced, she pleased Herod and his dinner guests. The king said to the girl, "Ask me for anything you want, and I'll give it to you." And he promised her with an oath, "Whatever you ask I will give you, up to half my kingdom"' (Mark 6:22–23). On that occasion a dark purpose and an evil design lay behind the proceedings. The favour demanded was 'give me right now the head of John the Baptist on a platter'. A prophet died and a king was doomed to the torment of conscience.

A modest request 5:4

Some have expressed surprise at Esther's apparent failure to grasp what seems a golden opportunity. Further reflection will reveal that she is again acting with great wisdom. Words are cheap and had Esther blurted out her nationality and requested the sparing of her people, the venture may well have failed. Haman is still all powerful and he, unlike her, has open access to the king. If she had followed this course of action, at best she would have been sidelined and Haman left in place to strike another day. At worst, Haman would have accused the Jews of treason or used some other device to have her, along with the Jews, slaughtered according to plan.

Her wisdom, of course, comes from God: 'Trust in the Lord with all your heart and lean not on your own understanding; in all your ways acknowledge him, and he will make your paths straight' (Prov. 3:5–6). The Lord is in no hurry; the timing of his purposes is perfect. All the pieces of his puzzle are not yet in place to achieve the destruction of Haman and the deliverance of his people. Esther is not slack but wise in her actions. 'Do you see a man who speaks in haste? There is more hope for a fool than for him' (Prov. 29:20). Less haste and more trust would often serve God's people well.

Pride before a fall 5:5–8

'Before his downfall a man's heart is proud, but humility comes before honour' (Prov. 18:12). Esther's inclusion of Haman in the invitation to her banquet is, humanly speaking, a stroke of genius. His pride is yet further inflated and any suspicions he may have entertained neutralised. Haman, to his great delight, is the sole guest at this banquet prepared by the beloved queen for her 'great king'. The occasion was obviously a huge success, tribute doubtless to the great care with which Esther had prepared everything. Over wine at the end of the feast the now intrigued Xerxes seeks once more to discover why his queen has sought him out at such risk to herself. Again, with wisdom and humility she replies, 'If the king regards me with favour and if it pleases the king to grant my petition and fulfil my request, let the king and Haman come tomorrow to the banquet I will prepare for them. Then I will answer the king's question' [5:8].

There is a very fine line between tantalising the king's inquisitiveness by this further delay and annoying him. The Lord ensures on which side of that line Esther's proposal falls. Her request is granted. Haman's pride is stoked yet further and the king filled with curiosity. God usually acts in accordance with his own laws of nature, not against them. Miracles are rarely unnatural, always supernatural. Notable exceptions are to be found in two biblical accounts: namely that of Joshua's prayer (Josh. 10) and Hezekiah's retreating shadow (2 Kings 20). Anticipation is often the enemy of sleep; few children sleep in on Christmas morning. Crucial to the next phase of God's plan is a sleepless night for Xerxes.

Approaching a far greater King

Before we leave this section, we must pause in the narrative to see the hidden lessons that are here to be learnt.

ACCESS TO THE KING

There were many reasons why access to earthly kings is never easy to obtain.

- They have limited time and energy and need to be preserved from unnecessary distractions.
- They must be protected from possible assassination.
- It is in the interests of their close advisors to limit their exposure to the views of others.

None of these considerations clearly apply to our heavenly King, yet Scripture makes it clear that access to his presence is also difficult. The structure of the Tabernacle and later the Temple[1] with their courts within courts was designed to restrict access. Only certain categories of people were allowed to progress through these barriers: Gentiles, women, Israelite men, and even priests—all had their cut-off point. At the centre stood the 'Most Holy Place' where only the High Priest could enter and that only under the strictest of conditions and the most specific of terms. The reason for his 'separation' is much more profound. Thomas Binney expresses it well in his hymn:

Eternal Light! Eternal Light!
How pure the soul must be,
When, placed within Thy searching sight,
It shrinks not, but with calm delight
Can live and look on Thee.

The spirits that surround Thy throne
May bear the burning bliss;
But that is surely theirs alone,
Since they have never, never known
A fallen world like this.

O how shall I, whose native sphere
Is dark, whose mind is dim,
Before the Ineffable appear,
And on my naked spirit bear
The uncreated beam?[2]

The issue and the burning question are well put. God is holy. When God delivered his Law at Sinai, the people were forbidden to let even an animal touch the mountain (Exod. 19:10–13). Joshua reminds the people of the great gulf that existed between them and this holy God and the attendant problem in serving him (Josh. 24:19). Nahum also called to mind the awesomeness of God: 'The mountains quake before him and the hills melt away. The earth trembles at his presence, the world and all who live in it' (Nahum 1:5). Scripture exhorts us to 'Ascribe to the Lord the glory due to his name. Bring an offering and come before him; worship the Lord in the splendour of his holiness. Tremble before him, all the earth! The world is firmly established; it cannot be moved' (1 Chron. 16:29–30).

But what offering can we bring? It is against this backdrop of God's unapproachable holiness that the present, amazing access of the Christian into God's presence must be viewed. Without this essential context our wonder will never be adequately felt. The extent and reason for that access is one dominant theme in the book of Hebrews:

> Therefore, brothers, since we have confidence to enter the Most Holy Place by the blood of Jesus, by a new and living way opened for us through the curtain, that is, his body, and since we have a great priest over the house of God, let us draw near to God with a sincere heart in full assurance of faith, having our hearts sprinkled to cleanse us from a guilty conscience and having our bodies washed with pure water.
>
> Hebrews 10:19–22

There was a graphic portrayal of this newfound freedom at the very moment it was made possible: 'And when Jesus had cried out again in a loud voice, he gave up his spirit. At that moment the curtain of the temple was torn in two from top to bottom. The earth shook and the rocks split' (Matt. 27:50–51). Christ's penal, substitutionary death on the cross satisfied the justice of a holy God and reconciled him to sinners (2 Cor. 5:18–21, Col. 1:22). Binney's hymn triumphantly ends:

There is a way for man to rise
To that sublime abode:
An offering and a sacrifice,
A Holy Spirit's energies.
An Advocate with God.

These, these prepare us for the sight
Of holiness above;
The sons of ignorance and night
Can dwell in the eternal Light,
Through the eternal Love.

ROBES FIT FOR A KING

Jesus told many parables about weddings. The final twist in one parable comes when the guests are expelled from the reception because they are not suitably dressed (Matt. 22:1–14). Clothes and social acceptability are often linked. Functions can be designated 'black tie', indicating that only formal dress is permissible. Many a seaside store in the UK sports the warning 'no swimwear'. Before tobacco advertising was banned on British television, the firm making 'Hamlet Cigars' produced a series of adverts that attained cult status. They portrayed various disasters in the midst of which the only comfort was, according to the slogan, 'Happiness is a Cigar called Hamlet'. One contribution to this series revolved around a man making a dramatic entrance, complete with sound effects, into a room dressed as a chicken. Imagine his consternation to discover that this was not the fancy dress party he expected but a very sober and formal affair!

No one would dream of attending a Royal Garden Party at Buckingham Palace dressed in jeans and a T-shirt, nor would the officials present permit them to do so. The question of how we should dress to approach God should not be trivialised into a mere discussion on the merits of wearing a suit to church on Sunday. That is a matter of culture, not right and wrong. There is, however, a significant issue to be considered.

Adam and Eve were, as created, clothed in innocence. They were naked and unashamed. An immediate consequence of their sin was that they sought to cover their newly found shame with garments made from fig leaves. This proved unacceptable to God who reclothed them in the skins of animals. God's action is noteworthy as it required the shedding of blood (Gen. 3).

The theme of the need for clothing is furthered in the elaborate instructions for the robes that priests must wear if they are to minister in the tabernacle (Exod. 28–29, 31, 35, Lev. 8, 16, 21). The spiritual meaning is seen clearly in such passages as Isaiah 64:6—'All of us have become like one who is unclean, and all our righteous acts are like filthy rags; we all shrivel up like a leaf, and like the wind our sins sweep us away.'

The salvation Christ secured for his people and their consequent acceptability to God is illustrated by the image of 'white robes'. The risen Christ urged the church in Laodicea to 'buy ... white clothes to wear, so that you can cover your shameful nakedness' (Rev. 3:18). The saints in heaven figure in a wonderful dialogue between John and 'one of the elders':

Then one of the elders asked me, 'These in white robes—who are they, and where did they come from?'

I answered, 'Sir, you know.'

And he said, 'These are they who have come out of the great tribulation; they have washed their robes and made them white in the blood of the Lamb. Therefore, they are before the throne of God

and serve him day and night in his temple;

and he who sits on the throne will spread his tent over them.

Never again will they hunger;

never again will they thirst.

The sun will not beat upon them,

nor any scorching heat.

For the Lamb at the centre of the throne will be their shepherd;

he will lead them to springs of living water.

And God will wipe away every tear from their eyes.

Revelation 7:13–17

The message is clear: man's efforts can never 'clothe' him in such a way that will enable him to stand before God. Only the death of Christ can achieve that access and acceptance.

AT THE RIGHT HAND OF THE KING

The right hand is the place of power, influence and authority. Such was the place occupied by Joseph in Egypt (Gen. 41:39), Daniel in Babylon (Dan. 6) and sadly Haman in Persia. When the Psalmist wished to express the truth that his life was willingly under the God's rule he wrote: 'I have set the Lord always before me. Because he is at my right hand, I shall not be shaken' (Ps. 16:8). It is the image used by the Lord Jesus to acknowledge his deity during his trial before the high priest: 'But Jesus remained silent and gave no answer. Again the high priest asked him, "Are you the Christ, the Son of the Blessed One?" "I am," said Jesus. "And you will see the Son of Man sitting at the right hand of the Mighty One and coming on the clouds of heaven"' (Mark 14:61–62).

Jesus quoted Psalm 110, where the Christ is pictured sitting at the right hand of God, to confound the Pharisees (Matt. 22:41–46). The same image informs Peter's gospel message (see also 1 Peter 3:22):

Peter and the other apostles replied: 'We must obey God rather than men! The God of our fathers raised Jesus from the dead —whom you had killed by hanging him on a tree. God exalted him to his own right hand as Prince and Saviour that he might give repentance and forgiveness of sins to Israel. We are witnesses of these things, and so is the Holy Spirit, whom God has given to those who obey him.'

Acts 5:29–32

Christ's exalted position at God's right hand is also the vision chosen to bring comfort to Stephen, the first Christian martyr, as he painfully departed from this present world (Acts 7:56). In the kingdoms ruled over by men, the power that evil men like Haman wield may for a while hold sway. Those kingdoms are, however, always subject to the final rule of Christ who, having completed his work of salvation, 'sat down at the right hand of the throne of the Majesty in heaven' (Heb. 8:1).

PETITIONING THE KING

Hymn writer, John Newton, both exhorts and encourages us with these words:

Thou art coming to a King,
Large petitions with thee bring;
For His grace and power are such,
None can ever ask too much.[3]

The last lesson we will seek to draw from this section concerns prayer. Metaphorically speaking, Christians are those to whom God's sceptre is extended and his gracious invitation made to bring their large petitions. Esther was there to seek the lives of her people. There is ample precedent for God's servant to petition him for the lives of others. Abraham famously pleaded for mercy on behalf of the inhabitants of Sodom and the other cities of the plain (Exod. 18:16–33). Moses asked God to 'blot him out' of the book of life rather than destroy Israel (Gen. 32:32). Paul could wish himself 'cursed and cut off', again for Israel's salvation. With such access to God and such encouragement to pray, what evidence is there in our churches of earnest pleading with God for the salvation of the lost?

Reflection/discussion topics from Chapter 8

1 How can we ensure that the balance between trusting God and using the very best human means to us is properly maintained?

2 Reflect on the prayers you have offered or heard recently and make a list of the types of petition made and their relative frequency. How do these compare with the prayers of the Apostle Paul? *Consider* Romans 1:8–12, 15:5–7, 15:13, 16:25–27; 1 Corinthians 1:4–7; 2 Corinthians 1:3–5, 12:7–10, 13:14; Ephesians 1:3, 1:8–12, 3:14–21; Philippians 1:8–11; Colossians 1:9–12; 1 Thessalonians 3:11–13, 5:23–24; 2 Thessalonians 1:11–12, 2:16–17, 3:5; 1 Timothy 1:17, 6:15–16 and Philemon 4–6.

3 What are the evidences of a 'proud heart'?

4 What would a humble man or woman look like? *Consider* Moses as an example (Num. 12:3).

5 Considering the costliness of our access into God's presence, what effect do you think it should have on the frequency, regularity and content of our prayer times?

6 What practical difference should it make to our lives to know that Christ is seated at God's right hand? *Read* Hebrews 8:1.

Notes

1 *The Illustrated Bible Dictionary,* volume 3 (Leicester: IVP, 1994), pp. 1522–1532.

2 **Thomas Binney,** 1798–1874, *Christian Hymns,* 5.

3 **John Newton,** 'Come my soul, thy suit prepare', *Christian Hymns,* 381.

No satisfaction

Esther 5:9–14

HAMAN'S RAGE AGAINST MORDECAI

9Haman went out that day happy and in high spirits. But when he saw Mordecai at the king's gate and observed that he neither rose nor showed fear in his presence, he was filled with rage against Mordecai. 10Nevertheless, Haman restrained himself and went home.

Calling together his friends and Zeresh, his wife, 11Haman boasted to them about his vast wealth, his many sons, and all the ways the king had honoured him and how he had elevated him above the other nobles and officials. 12'And that's not all,' Haman added. 'I'm the only person Queen Esther invited to accompany the king to the banquet she gave. And she has invited me along with the king tomorrow. 13But all this gives me no satisfaction as long as I see that Jew Mordecai sitting at the king's gate.'

14His wife Zeresh and all his friends said to him, 'Have a gallows built, seventy-five feet high, and ask the king in the morning to have Mordecai hanged on it. Then go with the king to the dinner and be happy.' This suggestion delighted Haman, and he had the gallows built.

A brief moment of joy 5:9

We turn once again to John Newton to set the scene for the next episode in this drama. In one of his hymns he pens these words:

Fading is the worldling's pleasure,
All his boasted pomp and show;
Solid joys and lasting treasure
None but Zion's children know.[1]

How aptly Haman illustrates this observation! Human psychology is such that we often swing between elation and depression. In its extreme form, this is commonly referred to as 'manic depression', but in milder forms it is ordinary human behaviour. Elijah is pitched into the deepest despair of his life immediately after his greatest triumph (1 Kings 18–19). Fresh from his victory over the prophets of Baal, it takes only a threat from Jezebel to make him despair of life itself. Depression in some degree is an experience known to most, if not all, of us. It is not uncommon for preachers to vow at the end of a difficult Sunday that they like Jeremiah 'will not mention him or speak any more in his name,' only to discover 'his word is in my heart like a fire, a fire shut up in my bones' (Jer. 20:9). The causes of depression can be many and varied; they may be genetic, physical, psychological, spiritual or a combination of these. On this occasion in Haman's case there was only one cause—sin.

The fly in the ointment 5:11–13

The fleeting joy Haman knew as a result of his unexpected favour in the queen's eyes was abruptly snatched away, when on his journey home, he passed Mordecai who once again failed to bow before him. Rage can take many forms, not merely the sudden loss of self-control commonly associated with it. In Haman's case it became a slow smouldering fire eating away at his soul. In the film *Star Trek 2, The Wrath of Khan,* Ricardo Montelbaum's character (Khan) tells Captain Kirk, 'Do you know there is a Klingon proverb which says, "Revenge is a dish best served cold." … it is very cold, in space.' Haman decided to take counsel and savour this particular dish at his leisure.

God made special provision in his Law to restrain human rage. He established cities of refuge to prevent the hot-blooded murder of someone who may have accidentally or unintentionally caused the death of another (Deut. 19:4–7). Paul includes 'fits of rage' in his list of the 'acts of the sinful nature': 'The acts of the sinful nature are obvious: sexual immorality, impurity and debauchery; idolatry and witchcraft; hatred, discord, jealousy, fits of rage, selfish ambition, dissensions, factions and envy; drunkenness, orgies, and the like. I warn you, as I did before, that those who live like this will not inherit the kingdom of God' (Gal. 5:19–21). He therefore commands the Colossian Christians to rid themselves of all such behaviour (Col. 3:8).

Fatal advice 5:14

Haman gathered together his friends and his wife to seek their advice. He began by boasting of all his many blessings and achievements, only to lament that it was all worthless so long as Mordecai was free to defy him We have already reflected on the danger of choosing bad counsellors. Haman is no better than his king; neither chose well those who would guide them. Zeresh, Haman's wife, earns a place in any 'wives' hall of infamy', along with Solomon's wives and Jezebel. Dishonourable mention perhaps ought also to be made of Job's wife. Satan first sought permission from God to attack Job, and then took from him his sons and daughters, his wealth and prestige, eventually even his health (Job 1–2). There is one exception to this comprehensive list of losses—Job's wife. The reason is soon apparent. She remains untouched because Satan intended to use her to tempt her husband into sin. She like Zeresh is the bringer of ungodly counsel: 'His wife said to him, "Are you still holding on to your integrity? Curse God and die!" He replied, "You are talking like a foolish woman. Shall we accept good from God, and not trouble?" In all this, Job did not sin in what he said' (Job 2:9–10).

It is only fair and just to record that there are also many examples in Scripture that illustrate the truth of Proverbs 18:22—'He who finds a wife finds what is good and receives favour from the Lord.' Nabal does not deserve the treasure he has in Abigail (1 Sam. 25), Ruth makes an exemplary companion for Boaz (Ruth), Hannah is both good and godly in the face of much provocation (1 Sam.1), and Ezekiel's wife is the 'delight of his eyes' (Ezek. 24:16). Clearly the choice of a wife (or husband) is a very important one.

There is an arrogance and presumption in both the advice given to and the action taken by Haman. The king was simply to rubberstamp these plans. So confident was Haman of his influence with the king that he did not even have the forethought to delay building the gallows until he had permission to kill his enemy. God hates presumption as he does all other manifestations of pride. Those who dare to append God's name to sanction their own imaginations are singled out for special condemnation: 'But a prophet who presumes to speak in my name anything I have not commanded him to say, or a prophet who speaks in the name of other gods, must be put to death' (Deut. 18:20). So are those who assume that God will sanction the plans they have made without bothering to pray.

Now listen, you who say, 'Today or tomorrow we will go to this or that city, spend a year there, carry on business and make money.' Why, you do not even know what will happen tomorrow. What is your life? You are a mist that appears for a little while and then vanishes. Instead, you ought to say, 'If it is the Lord's will, we will live and do this or that.' As it is, you boast and brag. All such boasting is evil.

James 4:13–16

This grisly monument of Haman's arrogance—the gallows—will eventually serve as a suitable instrument of his downfall.

Reflection/discussion topics from Chapter 9

1 The book of Ecclesiastes reflects at length on 'life without God' and concludes that it is meaningless. What things do people look to for meaning and joy? Do these things deliver what people hope for?

2 List the things in your life from which you expect meaning and joy. Are they different? *Consider* Matthew 6:25–34; Romans 2:7–11; Luke 16:13–14 and Hebrews 11.

3 Many Christians speak casually about having a 'quick temper'. Should this encourage complacency? *Consider* Proverbs 16:32, 15:1, 27:4, 29:11, 30:33; 1 Corinthians 12:20–21; Ephesians 4:26–32; Colossians 3:5–10; 1 Timothy 2:8 and James 1:19–21.

4 What consequences may follow from speaking and acting hastily? *Consider* Proverbs 29:20; Ecclesiastes 5:2 and 1 Timothy 5:22.

5 The modern term 'partner' is too ambiguous, and the expression 'spouse' somewhat archaic. So it may be wise to use a longhand expression and speak of husband and/or wife. What criteria should a Christian be looking for in a husband and/or wife?

6 *Consider* in general 1 Corinthians 7 and 2 Corinthians 6:14–17.

7 Why was Abraham so concerned in the story in Genesis 24?

8 Women, *consider* 1 Timothy 2:6; 1 Peter 1:5, 3:7; 1 John 2:14.

9 Men, *consider* 1 Timothy 2:9, 3:11; Titus 2:3–5 and 1 Peter 3:1–6.

Notes

1 **John Newton** 1725–1807, 'Glorious things of Thee are spoken', *Christian Hymns,* 333.

Belated gratitude

Esther 6:1–14

MORDECAI HONOURED

¹ That night the king could not sleep; so he ordered the book of the chronicles, the record of his reign, to be brought in and read to him. ² It was found recorded there that Mordecai had exposed Bigthana and Teresh, two of the king's officers who guarded the doorway, who had conspired to assassinate King Xerxes.

³ 'What honour and recognition has Mordecai received for this?' the king asked.

'Nothing has been done for him,' his attendants answered.

4 The king said, 'Who is in the court?' Now Haman had just entered the outer court of the palace to speak to the king about hanging Mordecai on the gallows he had erected for him.

⁵ His attendants answered, 'Haman is standing in the court.'

'Bring him in,' the king ordered.

⁶ When Haman entered, the king asked him, 'What should be done for the man the king delights to honour?'

Now Haman thought to himself, 'Who is there that the king would rather honour than me?' 7So he answered the king, 'For the man the king delights to honour, 8have them bring a royal robe the king has worn and a horse the king has ridden, one with a royal crest placed on its head. 9Then let the robe and horse be entrusted to one of the king's most noble princes. Let them robe the man the king delights to honour, and lead him on the horse through the city streets, proclaiming before him, "This is what is done for the man the king delights to honour!"'

10'Go at once,' the king commanded Haman. 'Get the robe and the horse and do just as you have suggested for Mordecai the Jew, who sits at the king's gate. Do not neglect anything you have recommended.'

¹¹So Haman got the robe and the horse. He robed Mordecai, and led him on horseback through the city streets, proclaiming before him, 'This is what is done for the man the king delights to honour!'

¹²Afterwards Mordecai returned to the king's gate. But Haman rushed home, with his head covered, in grief, ¹³and told Zeresh his wife and all his friends everything that had happened to him.

His advisers and his wife Zeresh said to him, 'Since Mordecai, before whom your downfall has started, is of Jewish origin, you cannot stand against him—you will surely come to ruin!' ¹⁴While they were still talking with him, the king's eunuchs arrived and hurried Haman away to the banquet Esther had prepared.

Deprived of sleep 6:1–6

The Psalmist attributes his good night's sleep to the following causes: 'I will lie down and sleep in peace, for you alone, O Lord, make me dwell in safety' (Ps. 4:8). ' In vain you rise early and stay up late, toiling for food to eat—for he grants sleep to those he loves' (Ps. 127:2).

The causes of insomnia vary as much as those of depression. All that concerns us here are the spiritual causes. A guilty conscience can certainly be one. When King Darius allowed himself to be manoeuvred into condemning his faithful servant to a gruesome death in the lion's den, it greatly disturbed him. He spent an anxious night before being able to release the miraculously preserved Daniel: 'Then the king returned to his palace and spent the night without eating and without any entertainment being brought to him. And he could not sleep' (Dan. 6:18).

On this auspicious night, God robbed Xerxes of sleep. Tossing and turning, instead of 'counting sheep', he decided to have his own court records read aloud to him. He listened to the annals of his own reign. This seemingly innocent nostalgia unearthed his neglected gratitude to Mordecai. Mordecai had done his king a great service but had never been rewarded. The unthinkable had happened and the king was anxious to put it right. As every florist knows and delights in, large neglects require large gestures of atonement. Seeking advice on what such a grand gesture might consist of, he turned to the recently arrived Haman, and posed the question, 'What should be done for the man the king delights to honour?'

Haman's pride had manufactured the trap into which he was about to fall. Now it pushed him headlong into it. He reasoned that the king could have only him in mind and so suggested the thing most pleasing to himself—a public show of honour unequalled in living memory. He sought an elevation that would give him quasi-kingly status. He piled honour upon honour: the king's clothes, his horse, a royal crest, a prince as escort and a herald to proclaim his glory. His mind was still dizzy with the sheer delight of it all when, like a bucket of iced water, he heard the words: '"Go at once," the king commanded Haman. "Get the robe and the horse and do just as you have suggested for Mordecai the Jew, who sits at the king's gate. Do not neglect anything you have recommended."'

Bitter obedience 6:10–12

There was no other course of action open to Haman than to swallow this bitter pill. The anguish those next hours must have caused him can hardly be imagined. Swallowing gall would have been preferable. Everything that he in his arrogance thought should be his, he was now compelled to lavish upon his bitterest enemy. Insult was added to injury. He was the author of his own humiliation—it was his idea. Former British Prime Minister Harold Wilson famously said 'a week is a long time in politics'. It is often repeated at times of crisis, and would certainly have struck a chord with Haman. The day had started so well; the gallows was complete and permission to hang Mordecai regarded as a mere formality. Then followed the banquet with Esther and the king; what could have been better? It had promised the perfect conclusion to a perfect day. Yet in a few short hours his bubble burst and he now knew only grief.

It is interesting, in the light of the impending edict, that Xerxes referred to Mordecai as 'the Jew' [6:10]. One likely explanation is that in keeping with his indifference shown in Esther 3:8, Xerxes even now had not bothered to inquire who exactly the 'certain people' are that he had condemned to annihilation.

Grief can have a very real physical effect on people, as it did now on Haman. Grief may come from many sources: family (Prov. 17:21), others' distress (Lam. 3:46–51), bad news (Matt. 17:23), even too much knowledge (Eccles. 1:18). God's people, however, can rest assured that their grief is temporary and will one day be utterly eclipsed by the wonders God is preparing for them (1 Pet.1:6, Rom. 8:1, Rev. 21:3). No such comfort awaits the ungodly. Like Haman, they can only wait to reap the whirlwind. 'Do not be deceived: God cannot be mocked. A man reaps what he sows. The one who sows to please his sinful nature, from that nature will reap destruction; the one who sows to please the Spirit, from the Spirit will reap eternal life' (Gal. 6:7–8).

A noteworthy contrast between Haman and Mordecai emerges at this point. While the day's events were crushing to the former, they seemed of little significance to the latter. The author simply records that Mordecai returned to his place of work—the gate. He did not have the proud disposition that would allow him to revel in this unforeseen glory. He is truly a man of humble and contrite heart, the kind of man that God loves. 'This is the one I esteem: he who is humble and contrite in spirit, and trembles at my word' (Isa. 66:2).

Doomed to destruction 6:13–14

Zeresh's reaction to Haman's humiliation is as fascinating to us as it must have been appalling to him. First, she predicted that her husband's inevitable downfall had already begun. Perhaps she acted as unconsciously as Caiaphas did when, after the raising of Lazarus, he uttered words merely expedient to himself but, in God's overruling, prophetic of salvation. 'You do not realise that it is better for you that one man die for the people than that the whole nation perish' (John 11:50).

Zeresh had given her proud husband his first clue that this day's events were not merely a setback to his plans but a harbinger of certain doom. She also saw not only his certain destruction but also its correct cause. It was not just his evil scheming; not even that he had plotted against a good man;

it lay in the fact that Mordecai was a Jew. Haman had lifted up his hand against the Almighty, and his doom was sealed.

God's protective love for his people is pictured in Zechariah 2:8—'For this is what the LORD Almighty says: … whoever touches you touches the apple of his eye.' Charles Spurgeon, that prince of preachers, commented on this verse by saying of God:

He esteems them as much as men value their eyesight, and is as careful to protect them from injury, as men are to protect the apple of their eye. The pupil of the eye is the tenderest part of the tenderest organ, and very fitly sets forth the inexpressible tenderness of God's love. As Calvin remarks, "There is nothing more delicate or more tender than the eye in the body of a man; for were one to bite my finger or prick my arm or my legs, or even severely to wound me, I should feel no such pain as by having the pupil of my eye injured." Behold, then, beloved, a mystery of loving kindness and affection. The Lord sitteth upon the circle of the earth, and the inhabitants thereof are as grasshoppers, the nations are as a drop of a bucket, and are counted as the small dust of the balance: how marvellous that he has thoughts of everlasting love towards such worthless things![1]

Time and again the Lord of hosts does battle on behalf of his people. Once again he stretches out his mighty arm to deliver. 'Surely the arm of the Lord is not too short to save, nor his ear too dull to hear' (Isa. 59:1).

How Zeresh became suddenly aware that her husband was playing with fire we are not told. Scripture records instances where the Lord's fame preceded him. A key element in Rahab's willingness to rescue Joshua's spies from the city of Jericho is found in her report of God's deeds. News of the crossing of the Red Sea and Israel's victory over the Amorites had already reached her ears (Josh. 2:9–11). The impact of the news was widespread for she reported that 'When we heard of it, our hearts sank and everyone's courage failed because of you, for the Lord your God is God in heaven above and on the earth below' (Josh. 2:11). A similar awe for God is shared by the sailors whom Jonah encounters during his abortive attempt to avoid preaching to the Ninevites. Their fear is engendered by the revelation that Jonah is 'running away from the LORD' (Jonah 1:1–10).

One way for God's 'fame' to spread is by the testimony of his people.

This exhortation is repeated in Scripture. The most famous of such exhortations is repeated three times in the Old Testament (1 Chron. 16:8, Ps. 105:1, Isa. 12:4) and alluded to by Paul in his letter to the Colossians (Col. 1:27): 'Give thanks to the LORD, call on his name; make known among the nations what he has done' (1 Chron. 16:8). It inspired Charles Wesley's well-known hymn:

You servants of God,
your master proclaim,
and tell out abroad his wonderful name;
the name all-victorious of Jesus extol,
his kingdom is glorious, and rules over all.[2]

No sooner had Zeresh delivered her portent of doom than the eunuchs arrived to conduct Haman to Esther's feast.

Reflection/discussion topics from Chapter 10

1 What is the relationship between conscience and guilt in the word of God? *Consider* Genesis 20:1–7; 1 Samuel 25; Acts 24:16; Romans 9:1; 1 Corinthians 4:1–5 and 1 Peter 3:13–18.

2 If you found yourself in Haman's position of (supposedly) choosing your own reward, what would you choose? What does that say about you? Would you be content if that reward were given to someone else?

3 'Persecution is the normal condition of the people of God.' How true do you think that is historically? How true is it today throughout the world? *Consider* Psalm 9:13, 119:161; Matthew 5:10–12, 10:23; Romans 8:35–36; 2 Corinthians 4:7–12; Hebrews 11:35–38 and Revelation 2:10–11.

4 The book of Esther demonstrates the favour of God towards his people. In what ways does he demonstrate this? *Consider* Isaiah 60:10; Proverbs 12:2; Psalm 5:12, 30:7, 44:3 and Job 10:12.

5 Whose responsibility is it to 'tell out abroad his wonderful name'?

6 *Consider* Deuteronomy 6:1–12; Psalm 9:10–12, 22:27–31, 40:9–13, 64:9–10, 92:1–2, 106:1–2; Isaiah 43:19–24; Matthew 28:16–20 and Acts 8:4.

7 *Consider* Colossians 4:4 as a prayer to adopt.

Chapter 10

Notes

1 **C.H. Spurgeon,** Metropolitan Tabernacle Pulpit Sermon No. 452, delivered on Sunday evening, April 27th, 1862.
2 **Charles Wesley,** 1707–88, this version from *Praise!* (Darlington: Praise Trust), 342.

The death of Haman

Esther 7:1–10

HAMAN HANGED

[1] So the king and Haman went to dine with Queen Esther, [2] and as they were drinking wine on that second day, the king again asked, 'Queen Esther, what is your petition? It will be given you. What is your request? Even up to half the kingdom, it will be granted.'

[3] Then Queen Esther answered, 'If I have found favour with you, O king, and if it pleases your majesty, grant me my life—this is my petition. And spare my people—this is my request. [4] For I and my people have been sold for destruction and slaughter and annihilation. If we had merely been sold as male and female slaves, I would have kept quiet, because no such distress would justify disturbing the king.'

[5] King Xerxes asked Queen Esther, 'Who is he? Where is the man who has dared to do such a thing?'

[6] Esther said, 'The adversary and enemy is this vile Haman.'

Then Haman was terrified before the king and queen. [7] The king got up in a rage, left his wine and went out into the palace garden. But Haman, realising that the king had already decided his fate, stayed behind to beg Queen Esther for his life.

[8] Just as the king returned from the palace garden to the banquet hall, Haman was falling on the couch where Esther was reclining.

The king exclaimed, 'Will he even molest the queen while she is with me in the house?'

As soon as the word left the king's mouth, they covered Haman's face. [9] Then Harbona, one of the eunuchs attending the king, said, 'A gallows seventy-five feet high stands by Haman's house. He had it made for Mordecai, who spoke up to help the king.'

The king said, 'Hang him on it!' ¹⁰So they hanged Haman on the gallows he had prepared for Mordecai. Then the king's fury subsided.

The queen's petition 7:1–4

The Teacher, son of David, king of Jerusalem (Eccles. 1:1) wisely observed that there is 'a time to tear and a time to mend, a time to be silent and a time to speak' (Eccles. 3:7). Esther knew that this was the time to speak. Xerxes' curiosity is at breaking point; Haman is no longer self-assured; all of God's pieces are in place.

Again we can marvel at Esther's wisdom. First, she asked for her own life. This must not be construed as selfishness on her part. In doing so she ensured that the king did not fail to grasp the personal implications of the wider pleas she was about to make. Secondly, she interceded for her people. She did not request half a kingdom for herself, rather that the king not lose a valuable component of his own realm. Finally she turned Haman's own words back on his head. If the fate of her people had been anything less than 'destruction and slaughter and annihilation' [4:8, 7:4] she would not have disturbed the king's peace. Mere slavery for her people and herself would not have warranted such an intervention. What they faced, she made clear, was nothing less than extermination.

There is an alternate translation of verse 4. The NIV renders it: 'For I and my people have been sold for destruction and slaughter and annihilation. If we had merely been sold as male and female slaves, *I would have kept quiet, because no such distress would justify disturbing the king*' (my italics). The renderings in the KJV and NASB are of similar import. The NKJV, however, casts a different light and emphasises the potential financial loss to the king: 'For we have been sold, my people and I, to be destroyed, to be killed, and to be annihilated. Had we been sold as male and female slaves, I would have held my tongue, *although the enemy could never compensate for the king's loss*' (my italics).

If this translation is to be preferred, as many commentators believe, then Esther is drawing Xerxes' attention to the pecuniary reality that, even the vast sum Haman has promised to the treasury, will fail to provide adequate reparation for the king's loss of revenue. As so often when there are differences in translation, we are not faced with an either/or situation. Both renderings contain wisdom which we can apply.

Plain speaking 7:6

In her reply to the king's question, Esther is a model of plain speaking. Social convention necessarily makes us careful with our words. There is a fine line to be drawn; many who pride themselves on being blunt are in fact nothing more than rude and boorish. To dress up offensiveness as a virtue does not make it any more acceptable. Such speech is surely one example of the 'foolish talk' the Apostle Paul warns us against (Eph. 5:4). Much better to follow the wisdom of Colossians 4:6—'Let your conversation be always full of grace, seasoned with salt, so that you may know how to answer everyone.'

Certainly there are occasions that demand bluntness though never rudeness. Esther's brevity and directness is a good model. The Bible records that after David had committed adultery with Bathsheba, Nathan the prophet appeared before him, with the heartrending tale of two men and a pet lamb. Having aroused the king's anger over the apparent injustice, he suddenly abandoned his fiction and exposed the king's sin in the simple words, 'You are the man!' (2 Sam. 12).

Similarly, Peter confronted sin in Ananias and Sapphira with the words, 'How is it that Satan has so filled your heart that you have lied to the Holy Spirit?' (Acts 5:3). And in Simon the Sorcerer with the words, 'May your money perish with you, because you thought you could buy the gift of God with money!' (Acts 8:20). As noted previously, in Galatians Peter found himself justifiably on the receiving end of Paul's plain speaking: 'When Peter came to Antioch, I opposed him to his face, because he was clearly in the wrong' (Gal. 2:11).

Wisdom would counsel caution. Our hearts can be extremely deceptive (Jer. 17:9) and Scripture on balance stresses curbing our tongues.

The king's wrath 7:7

Once again the king's anger is aroused, but this time his wrath is appropriate and justified. Anger is usually and rightly regarded as a sin. So the Apostle Paul wisely reminds the Ephesians of the wisdom of Psalm

4:4—'"In your anger do not sin"': 'Do not let the sun go down while you are still angry, and do not give the devil a foothold' (Eph. 4:26–27). There are certain occasions when anger can be a virtue rather than a vice. We see a clear example of this in the Lord Jesus throwing the moneychangers out of the Temple (Matt. 21:12–13). The Saviour was angered by the degrading of his 'Father's house' from a 'house of prayer' to a 'den of robbers'. He manifested his holy anger in an unmistakable manner, overturning their worktables and driving them out. Another example is young David's indignation at Goliath's arrogance in mocking the living God (1 Sam. 17).

In Scripture anger is clearly revealed as one of God's attributes and a motive for some of his actions. Because of God's anger, Israel was condemned to wander in the wilderness for forty years (Num. 32:10–13). Likewise God's anger, said to have been fierce (Deut. 29:22–29), lay behind the complete overthrow of Sodom, Gomorrah, Admah and Zeboiim. When David sought to bring the Ark of God up to Jerusalem, a man called Uzzah acted with reckless irreverence and touched the sacred chest. This action resulted in his immediate death at the hands of God (2 Sam. 6). Anger is not always wrong, and we like God should be angry over injustice, blasphemy and sin in all its manifestations. A cautionary note should nevertheless be sounded. God is perfect in all his motives and actions; man is not. Too often our anger is wrongly founded or inappropriately expressed. The weight of Scripture would urge us to restraint and caution rather than giving vent to what can so easily lead us into sin.

Haman's death 7:8–10

There seems an appropriate lack of all dignity in the final moments of this man whom Esther accurately described as 'vile'. Terrified at the certainty of his own imminent ruin, he took advantage of the king's brief absence to literally cast himself upon the queen for mercy. The returning Xerxes was further enraged at this unwarranted violation. Instantly Haman was laid hold of and, with his face covered in shame, dragged away to execution. The scope of his plan against Mordecai was clearly known in the palace for the king's attention was drawn to the gallows Haman had so recently erected. The sympathies of Harbona the eunuch are revealed in his statement: 'He had it made for Mordecai, *who spoke up to help the king*' [7:9, my emphasis]. We can therefore add Harbona's name to the growing list of friends that godly Esther had made in this pagan court.

Without delay Haman is hanged and justice is both done and seen to be done. The architect of the great evil is dead. The king is placated, but the danger is far from past. There remains the problem of the irrevocable nature of 'the Law of the Medes and the Persians'. The edict of destruction stands and cannot be simply rescinded.

Missed opportunities

One aspect of the lengthy timescale and complex method by which God secured Haman's downfall must not be missed. It is an example of the great truth that 'The Lord is not slow in keeping his promise, as some understand slowness. He is patient with you, not wanting anyone to perish, but everyone to come to repentance' (2 Peter 3:9). Scripture abounds in accounts of the repentance and conversion of the most unlikely people. Who but a prophet like Jonah would have imagined the remarkable events in Nineveh (Jonah 3)? Manasseh (2 Chron. 33:12–13) sits alongside the well-known story of the repentant thief (Luke 23:42–43) as eloquent testimony to God's gracious and forgiving nature. God provided a window of opportunity for Haman through Mordecai's elevation. Instead of rushing home to lick his wounds, Haman could have sought audience with the king, confessed the evil of his plan and begged for mercy. Truly the path to hell is littered with missed opportunities. Three times in a short compass of verses the writer of the letter to the Hebrews reminds his readers of Psalm 95:7–8—'Today, if you hear his voice, do not harden your hearts.'

Reflection/discussion topics from chapter 11

1 Esther's requests to King Xerxes were both brief and explicit. Do you think there are lessons to be drawn here in respect to intercessory prayer? *Consider* Ecclesiastes 5:2 and Matthew 6:7–14.

2 If concise intercession is not to degenerate into brief prayer times, what other elements should be part of our prayer life? *Consider* 2 Chronicles 20:18; Psalm 50:14, 89:5, 103:2; Daniel 6:10, 9:20–21 and Revelation 5:12.

3 *Consider* this statement, 'If our prayers are not specific, we cannot know if or when they have been answered.'

4 There is clearly no truth at all in the old proverb that ends 'words can never hurt me'. Words can be a powerful force for both good and evil. What principles should guide our speech? *Consider* Psalm 12:3, 34:13–14, 35:28, 37:30, 55:20–21; Proverbs 5:3–6, 8:13, 22:11, 28:3; 1 Timothy 4:11–12; Titus 2:7–8; 1 Peter 3:10, and especially James 3.

5 *Consider* the proposition 'God is the God of second chances'. See Jonah 3:1; 2 Corinthians 13:1–2 and Titus 3:10–11. What are the implications for my relationship with God and with other people? For a cautionary note, see Isaiah 7:13.

The edict of salvation

Esther 8:1–17

THE KING'S EDICT ON BEHALF OF THE JEWS

[1] That same day King Xerxes gave Queen Esther the estate of Haman, the enemy of the Jews. And Mordecai came into the presence of the king, for Esther had told how he was related to her. [2] The king took off his signet ring, which he had reclaimed from Haman, and presented it to Mordecai. And Esther appointed him over Haman's estate.

[3] Esther again pleaded with the king, falling at his feet and weeping. She begged him to put an end to the evil plan of Haman the Agagite, which he had devised against the Jews. [4] Then the king extended the gold sceptre to Esther and she arose and stood before him.

[5] 'If it pleases the king,' she said, 'and if he regards me with favour and thinks it the right thing to do, and if he is pleased with me, let an order be written overruling the dispatches that Haman son of Hammedatha, the Agagite, devised and wrote to destroy the Jews in all the king's provinces. [6] For how can I bear to see disaster fall on my people? How can I bear to see the destruction of my family?'

[7] King Xerxes replied to Queen Esther and to Mordecai the Jew, 'Because Haman attacked the Jews, I have given his estate to Esther, and they have hanged him on the gallows. [8] Now write another decree in the king's name on behalf of the Jews as seems best to you, and seal it with the king's signet ring—for no document written in the king's name and sealed with his ring can be revoked.'

[9] At once the royal secretaries were summoned—on the twenty-third day of the third month, the month of Sivan. They wrote out all Mordecai's orders to the Jews, and to the satraps, governors and nobles of the 127 provinces stretching from India to Cush. These orders were written in the script of each province and the language of each people and also to the Jews in their own script and language. [10] Mordecai wrote in the name of King Xerxes, sealed the dispatches with the king's signet ring, and sent them by mounted couriers, who rode fast horses especially bred for the king.

¹¹The king's edict granted the Jews in every city the right to assemble and protect themselves; to destroy, kill and annihilate any armed force of any nationality or province that might attack them and their women and children; and to plunder the property of their enemies. ¹²The day appointed for the Jews to do this in all the provinces of King Xerxes was the thirteenth day of the twelfth month, the month of Adar. ¹³A copy of the text of the edict was to be issued as law in every province and made known to the people of every nationality so that the Jews would be ready on that day to avenge themselves on their enemies.

¹⁴The couriers, riding the royal horses, raced out, spurred on by the king's command. And the edict was also issued in the citadel of Susa.

¹⁵Mordecai left the king's presence wearing royal garments of blue and white, a large crown of gold and a purple robe of fine linen. And the city of Susa held a joyous celebration. ¹⁶For the Jews it was a time of happiness and joy, gladness and honour. ¹⁷In every province and in every city, wherever the edict of the king went, there was joy and gladness among the Jews, with feasting and celebrating. And many people of other nationalities became Jews because fear of the Jews had seized them.

Just reward 8:1–2

'A good man leaves an inheritance for his children's children, but a sinner's wealth is stored up for the righteous' (Prov. 13:22). One great theme of Scripture is that of rewards. They are used as a gracious means of encouragement to God's people; as in the case of David (2 Sam. 22:25), and Azariah (2 Chron. 15:1–7). Rewards play a part in the coming of God among his people (Isa. 40:10) and of the return of the Lord Jesus Christ (Rev. 22:12). We are made aware that these rewards are not always received in full during this earthly life: 'And everyone who has left houses or brothers or sisters or father or mother or children or fields for my sake will receive a hundred times as much and will inherit eternal life' (Matt. 19:29). Indeed, we are encouraged to view everything in the light of eternity: 'I consider that our present sufferings are not worth comparing with the glory that will be revealed in us' (Rom. 8:18). While it is not his norm, the Lord occasionally sees fit to reward in this world as well as in the next, and to do so materially as well as spiritually. Such was the case with Abraham and Lot (Gen. 13:5–6), Isaac (Gen. 26:12), Job (Job 42:12–17) and many others. It is not always so.

One modern dictionary[1] defines 'juxtaposition' as 'to place or situate side by side or close together, especially so as to produce or exhibit a contrasting effect'. There is a wonderful example of this literary device in Hebrews 11:33–39. Having spoken of many of the great men and women of faith who occupy the pages of Scripture, the writer, short on time proceeds to the army of unnamed 'heroes of faith'. First we read of those 'who through faith conquered kingdoms, administered justice, and gained what was promised; who shut the mouths of lions, quenched the fury of the flames, and escaped the edge of the sword; whose weakness was turned to strength; and who became powerful in battle and routed foreign armies. Women received back their dead, raised to life again' (Heb. 11:33–35).

These indeed seem fitting rewards for such faithful men and women. Then abruptly, in the middle of verse 35, the whole scene is transformed in an instant. Now we have a far less pleasing scenario: 'Others were tortured and refused to be released, so that they might gain a better resurrection. Some faced jeers and flogging, while still others were chained and put in prison. They were stoned; they were sawn in two; they were put to death by the sword. They went about in sheepskins and goatskins, destitute, persecuted and ill-treated—the world was not worthy of them. They wandered in deserts and mountains, and in caves and holes in the ground.'

We cannot mistake the writer's intent in setting these two very different outcomes side by side. His device of 'juxtaposition' is deliberately used to achieve maximum effect. He reminds us that 'These were all commended for their faith' (Heb. 11:39a). Rewards are not guaranteed in this world, though amazingly, they are in the world to come. If they come it is grace upon grace: we have no right to them, and we are not owed them by God.

The people of God are to hold material things with a very loose grip, a lesson Martin Luther learned well and incorporated in his well-known hymn 'A safe stronghold our God is still':

And though they take our life,
Goods, honour, children, wife,

Yet is their profit small:
These things shall vanish all;
The city of God remaineth.²

A rather dubious tradition attributes the writing of this hymn to the period of great danger before the Diet of Worms in April 1521, and has the great Reformer singing it as he enters the city.³ Whatever the historical context, its message struck a chord with the suffering Protestants and it was soon established as a great favourite and deserves to be such still.

A change of authority 8:2

The sovereign God chose in his grace to give to Mordecai all that once belonged to fallen Haman. Not only his wealth, but also his power and influence now rested in the hands of a man of God. This reversal of roles is a prelude to the final great change that will take place at the last judgement. Jesus teaches role reversal in his parable about the rich man and Lazarus (Luke 16:19–31). In the book of Revelation it is those who have abused wealth and power who are pictured weeping and wailing (Rev. 18). In glorious contrast, the beleaguered persecuted people of God enjoy perfect rest (Rev. 7:9–17).

By grace it is the destiny of God's people to sit on thrones (Rev. 3:21) and share the judgement with Christ (Rev. 20:4–6) instead of suffering the wrath of God (Rom. 8:1). In time Mordecai experienced such a transformation as will be the lot of every Christian in eternity.

The petition elaborated 8:3–6

There is considerable debate concerning the correct chronological place of verse 3. Did these events follow immediately after the banquet at which Haman was condemned or do they belong to a later occasion? The passage seems to suggest a more formal setting than Esther's royal apartments. It seems unlikely that the king would carry his 'golden sceptre' to a meal with his wife. The most likely scenario seems to be that the momentous events of the day we have just been studying had not permitted the lengthy explanation that the king would certainly demand. Consider what had already occurred:

- During the late night or early morning the king learns that Mordecai's report of the assassination attempt has gone without reward.
- He asks Haman who has arrived (to request the king to hang Mordecai) what he should do for the man whom he desires to honour.
- Haman, thinking that the king is referring to him, elaborates his wishes.
- The king commands him to honour Mordecai in the exact manner he has suggested.
- Later that morning Haman leads Mordecai in his ride of honour.
- Mordecai returns to the royal court while Haman goes home and complains to his wife and friends, who foretell his doom.
- Immediately the king's servants arrive to bring Haman to Esther's banquet.
- Early that afternoon Esther's second banquet takes place, at the end of which Haman is unmasked.
- Haman is led away and executed.
- In the late afternoon/early evening the king gives Esther all of Haman's property.
- Esther informs the king of her relationship to Mordecai who then joins them.
- The king gives Mordecai his newly reclaimed signet ring, and places him over Esther's recently acquired estate.

By any standards this is a busy day, which would be fully understandable why further petition is delayed until a later occasion, probably the next day.

The hand of God is clearly at work and Mordecai now has the right to enter the king's throne room, where Esther can also be confident of a warm welcome. This time the extending of the sceptre is little more than an anticipated formality. Indeed, she may well have come by previous agreement. Now Esther gives vent to the full extent of her emotion. She sets aside all formality and dignity and weeps at the king's feet. Here is passionate intercession of a kind too rarely heard (Rom. 9:1–3). If such humility is appropriate before an earthly monarch how much more before the King of kings!

Approach, my soul, the mercy-seat,
Where Jesus answers prayer;
There humbly fall before His feet,
For none can perish there.4

Such earnest seeking of God does not go unrewarded: 'Away from me, all you who do evil, for the Lord has heard my weeping. The Lord has heard my cry for mercy; the Lord accepts my prayer. All my enemies will be ashamed and dismayed; they will turn back in sudden disgrace' (Ps. 6:8–10). 'He who goes out weeping, carrying seed to sow, will return with songs of joy, carrying sheaves with him' (Ps. 126:6). 'The hearts of the people cry out to the Lord. O wall of the Daughter of Zion, let your tears flow like a river day and night; give yourself no relief, your eyes no rest' (Lam. 2:18).

As the deer pants for streams of water,
so my soul pants for you, O God.
My soul thirsts for God, for the living God.
When can I go and meet with God?
My tears have been my food
day and night,
while men say to me all day long,
'Where is your God?'
These things I remember
as I pour out my soul:
how I used to go with the multitude,
leading the procession to the house of God,
with shouts of joy and thanksgiving
among the festive throng.
Why are you downcast, O my soul?
Why so disturbed within me?
Put your hope in God,
for I will yet praise him,
my Saviour and my God.

Psalm 42:1–5

Pleading before the throne

Esther's intercession on behalf of her people had two main elements. She began and ended her prayer by pleading her own standing and favour before the king. Between these bookends lay the king's good pleasure.

Scripture sets the Lord Jesus Christ before us as, among other things, the great intercessor. 'Therefore he is able to save completely those who come to God through him, because he always lives to intercede for them' (Heb. 7:25). The elements noted above fill us with assurance and hope that Christ's intercession for us will certainly prevail. He is, after all, the Father's well-loved son. At key moments during his earthly ministry heaven invaded earth with verbal assurance: 'And a voice from heaven said, "This is my Son, whom I love; with him I am well pleased"' (Matt. 3:17; see also Matt. 17:5). Jesus expressed unbounded confidence as he stood before the grave of Lazarus; he prayed aloud purely for the sake of his audience: 'I knew that you always hear me, but I said this for the benefit of the people standing here, that they may believe that you sent me' (John 11:42).

The resurrection affirms that the Father has accepted the death of his Son as sufficient to meet the needs of his people. His mission is successfully completed to the utter satisfaction of the one who sent him. We can share the confidence expressed by Charitie Lees Chenez when she writes:

Before the throne of God above
I have a strong, a perfect plea,
A great High Priest, whose Name is Love,
Who ever lives and pleads for me.[5]

We may have confidence as well that our well-being is the Father's good pleasure: 'Do not be afraid, little flock, for your Father has been pleased to give you the kingdom' (Luke 12:32; see also Matt. 11:26, Luke 10:21, Eph. 1:9). 'As for the saints who are in the land, they are the glorious ones in whom is all my delight' (Ps. 16:3).

An unchangeable decree 8:7–8

We live in a world that is expert at duplicity. We no longer speak of telling lies but of being 'economical with the truth' or better still 'perpetrating a terminological inexactitude'. The Persians prided themselves on their infallibility. Why would they ever want to repeal a law? To do so admitted that it was imperfect when it had been passed. They therefore became past masters at circumvention. It is to this strategy that they now had to turn. True to character, Xerxes again evaded responsibility and passed the buck. Having abdicated his power once to Haman, he did so again, but this time to Mordecai and Esther.

The second edict 8:9–14

The edict that is passed is essentially one of authorising Jewish self-defence. It is not open to the accusation levelled by some that it made the Jews no better than their enemies. They were given the following rights:

- to gather in armed assembly
- to defend themselves against any and all armed forces that might attack them
- to utterly destroy such attackers
- to plunder their goods.

The wisdom and justice of this edict is clear—the onus now rests on their enemies. They have the legal right to attack the Jews, yet they are made aware of the potential consequences. If greed or hatred persuade them to avail themselves of this opportunity they may do so, but they must assume the risks. If wisdom prevails then peace is assured. If there is no attack there will be no reprisal. They are the architects of their own destiny. Once again we see God mercifully leaves open the door to repentance. Sadly once again men sin away the day of grace.

The urging of Ecclesiastes could not have been more apposite: 'Do not be overwicked, and do not be a fool—why die before your time?' (Eccles. 7:17). In his dealings with sinful men, under threat of his righteous judgement, God makes the same plea: 'Rid yourselves of all the offences you have committed, and get a new heart and a new spirit. Why will you die, O house of Israel? For I take no pleasure in the death of anyone, declares the Sovereign Lord. Repent and live!' (Ezek. 18:31–32). If any message echoes down the centuries from this sad and sorry history it is surely this one: 'Why will you die? Repent and live!'

The news of this edict of salvation for the Jews and invitation to life for their enemies was dispatched without delay throughout the empire. The Christian church is the custodian of a similar yet far greater edict—the gospel of our Lord Jesus Christ. It is a source of consternation that it is published with little enthusiasm and haste. Little wonder the hymn writer exhorts us:

Go quickly, for the fading hours
With haste are sinking to the west;
Exert with zeal thy ransomed powers,
Nor think it yet the time for rest.

Go quickly, for the sons of time
Are journeying to a hopeless grave,
And tell to earth's remotest clime
Of Him who came to seek and save.

Go quickly to the realms of sin;
Invite as many as you find;
And welcome all to enter in—
The poor, the maimed, the halt, the blind.

Go quickly with the living Word
Sent to the nations from above,
Till every heart on earth has heard
The tidings of redeeming love.[6]

Mordecai exalted again 8:15

There seems no end to the favours that Xerxes intended to shower upon Mordecai. The height of Haman's ambition was that for one day he might wear royal robes and receive adoration and homage. Here God's humble servant, without ever seeking anything for himself, is honoured in a far greater way. Each of the elements mentioned are of royal significance: the blue-and-white garments, the large golden crown and the purple robe all speak of royal dignity. These seem not to have been the gift of the king for a day but the permanent mark of new rank and dignity.

We have already noted the glorious robes in which the Apostle John sees the saints dressed (Rev. 7:13–14). In many ways this was prefigured in Zechariah 3:3–5:

Now Joshua was dressed in filthy clothes as he stood before the angel. The angel said to those who were standing before him, 'Take off his filthy clothes.' Then he said to Joshua, 'See, I have taken away your sin, and I will put rich garments on you.'

Then I said, 'Put a clean turban on his head.' So they put a clean turban on his head and clothed him, while the angel of the Lord stood by.

Each and every child of God can look forward to the day when they will forever cast away their own filthy rags (Isa. 64:6) to be dressed in robes of righteousness provided by God (Rev. 19:7–8).

A time of joy 8:16–17

The celebration among God's people recorded in verse 17 is what one would expect. Once the sentence of death was lifted the prospect of peace and prosperity lay before them. It is right and fitting to rejoice at such a time. The father of the prodigal had to point this out to his elder son in the story Jesus told (Luke 15:31). The joyless nature of much of our worship might indicate that the lesson has yet to be learned by many Christians. Pure joy derives from an appreciation of salvation: it is not emotionalism but it certainly is emotional. When David danced before the Lord as the Ark entered Jerusalem, it was not the result of some choreographed innovation, it was an expression of sheer unbounded delight in God (2 Sam. 6:13–15). In the early church that same delight expressed itself just as passionately:

They devoted themselves to the apostles' teaching and to the fellowship, to the breaking of bread and to prayer. Everyone was filled with awe, and many wonders and miraculous signs were done by the apostles. All the believers were together and had everything in common. Selling their possessions and goods, they gave to anyone as he had need. Every day they continued to meet together in the temple courts. They broke bread in their homes and ate together with glad and sincere hearts, praising God and enjoying the favour of all the people. And the Lord added to their number daily those who were being saved.

Acts 2:42–47

This passage from Acts highlights another similarity, the effect on those nearby. The events recounted in Esther heralded a new wave of conversions to Judaism. Some conversions might have been like those of so-called 'rice Christians', but undoubtedly many were genuine. The visible blessing of God on his people is often the catalyst for conversion. Read some of the many accounts of revival and your doubts will be removed.7 It was just how the Bereans (Acts 17:11–12) and the Corinthians (Acts 18:8) responded to the preaching of the Apostle Paul.

Reflection/discussion topics from Chapter 12

1 Seeking a reward has often been portrayed by Christians as an 'impure motive'. Is this a biblical perspective? *Consider* Hebrews 11:13–16, 26 and 12:2.

2 If we are not to seek rewards, why are we promised them? *Consider* Matthew 5:12, 6:4, 10:41–42; 1 Corinthians 3:8; Colossians 3:22–24; Hebrews 11:6 and 2 John 8.

3 How much should our expectation of future glory affect the way we live today? *Consider* Romans 8:18; 2 Thessalonians 1:5–10; 2 Timothy 2:9–13, 4:6–8 and Hebrews 10:32.

4 What is the difference between 'emotion' and 'emotionalism'? How can we promote the one while guarding against the other?

5 What active steps are you involved in so far as promoting the Gospel is concerned?

6 Are you involved in any way in 'world mission'?

7 Are you involved in any way with local evangelism? Perhaps through the outreach of your church?

8 When did you last witness verbally and personally to Christ?

9 Martin Luther once said, 'I would not give one moment of heaven for all the joy and riches of' the world, even if it lasted for thousands and thousands of years.' Does your life give evidence that you agree with him?

Chapter 12

Notes

1 *Universal Dictionary* (Readers' Digest, 1998).
2 **Martin Luther,** 1483–1546, 'A safe stronghold our God is still', *Christian Hymns,* 168.
3 http://www.luther.de/en/worms.html
4 **John Newton,** 1725–1807, *Christian Hymns*, 378.
5 **Charitie Lees Chenez,** 'Before the throne of God above', *Christian Hymns*, 258.
6 **William Wileman,** 1848–1944, *Christian Hymns*, 442.
7 Suggested reading includes **Brian Edwards,** *Revival: A people saturated with God* (Darlington: Evangelical Press), and **Stanley Griffin,** *A Forgotten Revival* (Epsom: DayOne Publications).

An empire in turmoil

Esther 9:1–17

TRIUMPH OF THE JEWS

¹ On the thirteenth day of the twelfth month, the month of Adar, the edict commanded by the king was to be carried out. On this day the enemies of the Jews had hoped to overpower them, but now the tables were turned and the Jews got the upper hand over those who hated them. ²The Jews assembled in their cities in all the provinces of King Xerxes to attack those seeking their destruction. No one could stand against them, because the people of all the other nationalities were afraid of them. ³And all the nobles of the provinces, the satraps, the governors and the king's administrators helped the Jews, because fear of Mordecai had seized them. ⁴Mordecai was prominent in the palace; his reputation spread throughout the provinces, and he became more and more powerful.

⁵The Jews struck down all their enemies with the sword, killing and destroying them, and they did what they pleased to those who hated them. ⁶In the citadel of Susa, the Jews killed and destroyed five hundred men. ⁷They also killed Parshandatha, Dalphon, Aspatha, ⁸Poratha, Adalia, Aridatha, ⁹Parmashta, Arisai, Aridai and Vaizatha, ¹⁰the ten sons of Haman son of Hammedatha, the enemy of the Jews. But they did not lay their hands on the plunder.

¹¹The number of those slain in the citadel of Susa was reported to the king that same day. ¹²The king said to Queen Esther, 'The Jews have killed and destroyed five hundred men and the ten sons of Haman in the citadel of Susa. What have they done in the rest of the king's provinces? Now what is your petition? It will be given you. What is your request? It will also be granted.'

¹³ If it pleases the king,' Esther answered, 'give the Jews in Susa permission to carry out this day's edict tomorrow also, and let Haman's ten sons be hanged on gallows.'

¹⁴So the king commanded that this be done. An edict was issued in Susa, and they hanged the ten sons of Haman. ¹⁵The Jews in Susa came together on the fourteenth day

of the month of Adar, and they put to death in Susa three hundred men, but they did not lay their hands on the plunder.

[16]Meanwhile, the remainder of the Jews who were in the king's provinces also assembled to protect themselves and get relief from their enemies. They killed seventy-five thousand of them but did not lay their hands on the plunder. [17]This happened on the thirteenth day of the month of Adar, and on the fourteenth they rested and made it a day of feasting and joy.

The tables are turned 9:1–7

Critics of the Bible are always swift to grasp any seeming contradiction in the inspired record. Invariably, as J W Haley deals with at length in his work *Alleged Discrepancies of the Bible*,[1] these are often founded on a shallow reading of the text. There is no real discrepancy between the Edict for Defence [8:11] and the statement in verse 2 that Jews assembled 'to attack' their enemies. Reconciliation of these statements follows immediately afterwards in the phrase 'those seeking their destruction'. Note the use of the present tense 'seeking' not the past tense 'sought'. The people who perished that day were those who attempted to carry out the first Edict of Destruction. Their downfall was of their own making; the Jews did not shed innocent blood. Our attention is also drawn to the fact that it was men who died; there does not seem to have been a slaughter of women and children. This contrasts with what Haman wanted to unleash on the Jews. The edict had granted this right [8:11], but it does not seem to have been exercised.

Particular mention is made of the ten sons of Haman who clearly used the day to seek to avenge the death of their father and reverse their own consequent impoverishment. As dreadful as that day must have been, it was not turned into a bloodbath. The death toll of 500 is far smaller than vengeance might have exacted. The much larger empire-wide total of 75,000 dead must itself be seen in light of the vastness of Xerxes' domain. Remember his proud boast 'I am Xerxes, the great king, the only king, the king of [all] countries [which speak] all kind of languages, the king of this [entire] big and far-reaching earth.' Neither is it necessary to see vindictiveness in Esther's subsequent petition. Her request to extend the battle for one more day, coupled as it is with the public display of the corpses of Haman's sons, easily bears a far different interpretation. As any gardener knows, unless a weed is taken out root and all it will reappear in a short time. The same is true of evil. The public exhibiting of executed felons, common in most civilisations until recent days, was intended as a prolonged warning to others to mend the error of their ways.

The Apostle Paul warns Timothy of the consequences of not dealing with the underlying causes of sin in our lives. 'People who want to get rich fall into temptation and a trap and into many foolish and harmful desires that plunge men into ruin and destruction. For the love of money is a root of all kinds of evil. Some people, eager for money, have wandered from the faith and pierced themselves with many griefs' (1 Tim. 6:9–10).

How fitting that those to whom God has shown such great mercy should themselves be merciful to others. They see themselves described in Toplady's well-known phrase as 'debtors to mercy alone'.[2] The dangers of any other attitude on the part of God's people are clearly spelt out in Jesus' parable about the unforgiving servant (Matt. 18:21–35). It is worth pondering this petition in the Lord's Prayer before expressing it as our own: 'Forgive us our debts, as we also have forgiven our debtors' (Matt. 6:12). Is this really what we intend to ask of God?

No plunder 9:8–17

Nothing is drawn to our attention in Scripture without purpose. This is the reason why a close study of the text will always yield fresh insight, however familiar we are with the passage. Why then are we twice informed that on this day of opportunity the Jews took no plunder? The Edict specifically permitted such action which would have been in keeping with common practice. The Jews, however, have a nobler precedent at the dawn of their history.

Genesis 14 tells the story of battle between two coalitions of kings. On the one side 'Kedorlaomer king of Elam, Tidal king of Goiim, Amraphel king of Shinar and Arioch king of Ellasar' on the other stood 'the king of Sodom, the king of Gomorrah, the king of Admah, the king of Zeboiim and the king of Bela (that is, Zoar)' 'four kings against five'. The result was defeat for the king of Sodom and his allies.

As might be expected, the victors plundered the cities of the vanquished and 'they also carried off Abram's nephew Lot and his possessions, since he was living in Sodom'. It is testimony to Abram's wealth and power at this time that he is able to assemble a sufficient military force to pursue Kedorlaomer, recover the spoil and liberate Lot. In gratitude the king of Sodom seeks to strike a bargain. It is not the generous gesture it may at first seem: his proposal is that Abram keep the goods while returning the people to the king. Both of course now belonged to Abram as spoils of war and the king of Sodom was in no position to take anything by force. His offer is an opening gambit in a negotiation, which he hopes will reduce his losses. Abram's response must have taken him utterly by surprise. He refuses to take anything, either people or goods. His reason for this remarkable decision follows: 'But Abram said to the king of Sodom, "I have raised my hand to the Lord, God Most High, Creator of heaven and earth, and have taken an oath that I will accept nothing belonging to you, not even a thread or the thong of a sandal, so that you will never be able to say, 'I made Abram rich'"' (Gen. 14:22–23). The Jews, like their father Abraham, seek no gain from the hands of sinners.

Reflection/discussion topics from chapter 13

1 What do you think of the following definition: 'Mercy is God not giving us what we do deserve, while grace is him giving us what we do not deserve'?

2 Read *Grace—Amazing Grace* by Brian Edwards (Leominster: Day One Publications), especially Chapter 9 'Forgiving Grace'.

3 In our striving to deal with sin in our own lives, are we getting at the roots or just hacking away at the branches?

4 What principles will help us know the difference? *Consider* Matthew 5:27–30, 19:16–25; 1 Timothy 6:10 and 2 Timothy 4:10.

5 Do the examples of Abraham and Esther have lessons to teach us about wealth?

6 Are there acceptable and unacceptable ways of gaining wealth?

7 What should the Christian's attitude be to such things as lotteries?

8 *Consider* Genesis 14 and Esther 9: 8, 15.

Notes

1 First edition 1874 (Grand Rapids: Baker Book House, 1977 reprint).

2 Augustas Toplady, 1740–78, *Christian Hymns* (Bridgend: Evangelical Movement of Wales, 1977), 566.

The great celebration

Esther 9:18–10:3

PURIM CELEBRATED

^{18}The Jews in Susa, however, had assembled on the thirteenth and fourteenth, and then on the fifteenth they rested and made it a day of feasting and joy.

^{19}That is why rural Jews—those living in villages—observe the fourteenth of the month of Adar as a day of joy and feasting, a day for giving presents to each other.

^{20}Mordecai recorded these events, and he sent letters to all the Jews throughout the provinces of King Xerxes, near and far, ^{21}to have them celebrate annually the fourteenth and fifteenth days of the month of Adar ^{22}as the time when the Jews got relief from their enemies, and as the month when their sorrow was turned into joy and their mourning into a day of celebration. He wrote to them to observe the days as days of feasting and joy and giving presents of food to one another and gifts to the poor.

^{23}So the Jews agreed to continue the celebration they had begun, doing what Mordecai had written to them. ^{24}For Haman son of Hammedatha, the Agagite, the enemy of all the Jews, had plotted against the Jews to destroy them and had cast the pur (that is, the lot) for their ruin and destruction. ^{25}But when the plot came to the king's attention, he issued written orders that the evil scheme Haman had devised against the Jews should come back on to his own head, and that he and his sons should be hanged on the gallows. ^{26}(Therefore these days were called Purim, from the word pur.) Because of everything written in this letter and because of what they had seen and what had happened to them, ^{27}the Jews took it upon themselves to establish the custom that they and their descendants and all who join them should without fail observe these two days every year, in the way prescribed and at the time appointed. ^{28}These days should be remembered and observed in every generation by every family, and in every province and in every city. And these days of Purim should never cease to be celebrated by the Jews, nor should the memory of them die out among their descendants.

^{29}So Queen Esther, daughter of Abihail, along with Mordecai the Jew, wrote with full authority to confirm this second letter concerning Purim. [30]And Mordecai sent letters to all the Jews in the 127 provinces of the kingdom of Xerxes—words of goodwill and assurance—[31]to establish these days of Purim at their designated times, as Mordecai the Jew and Queen Esther had decreed for them, and as they had established for themselves and their descendants in regard to their times of fasting and lamentation. [32]Esther's decree confirmed these regulations about Purim, and it was written down in the records.

THE GREATNESS OF MORDECAI

[1] King Xerxes imposed tribute throughout the empire, to its distant shores. [2]And all his acts of power and might, together with a full account of the greatness of Mordecai to which the king had raised him, are they not written in the book of the annals of the kings of Media and Persia? [3]Mordecai the Jew was second in rank to King Xerxes, pre-eminent among the Jews, and held in high esteem by his many fellow Jews, because he worked for the good of his people and spoke up for the welfare of all the Jews.

A lasting memorial 9:18–32

As we reach the very end of this wonderful book, we are let into the secret of why it was first written. It was there not just as a record of these momentous events but as an explanation of why the Jews had taken the unprecedented step of adding a feast to those ordained by Moses. The justification for the existence of the feast and the manner of its celebration are set down for the benefit of future generations.

Some have questioned if it is appropriate to celebrate something that involved the shedding of so much blood. Their celebration, like those of the Allies in the Second World War on VE and VJ Days, were of victory and deliverance not of the bloodshed to secure them.

The book of Revelation tells of a day, yet to come, when the people of God will celebrate a far greater and more permanent victory:

When they see the smoke of her burning, they will exclaim, 'Was there ever a city like this great city?' They will throw dust on their heads, and with weeping and mourning cry out:

'Woe! Woe, O great city,
where all who had ships on the sea
became rich through her wealth!
In one hour she has been brought to ruin!
Rejoice over her, O heaven!
Rejoice, saints and apostles and prophets!
God has judged her for the way she treated you.'

Revelation 18:18–20

The Jews had biblical precedent for marking such occasions. Joshua had set up stones to mark the site of the crossing of the Jordan with the express purpose that 'these stones are to be a memorial to the people of Israel for ever'. Many of the treasures that fill our museums and adorn our city streets are memorials in stone to one victory or another. The feast was to be a living memorial, an annual remembrance perpetuated by the Jews, lest they forget.

It is salutary to remember just how prone to forgetfulness we are, even of the mighty deeds of our God. If you own a concordance look up the word 'remember' and see just how often God has to exhort his people to do just that. Psalm 136 is a responsive psalm in which the acts of God are rehearsed in order that the people can respond 'His love endures for ever'. At the heart of the Christian faith is the Communion service in which the finished work of Christ on the cross is remembered and celebrated. The earliest account of this, given by the Apostle Paul in his letter to the Corinthians, contains these significant words 'in remembrance of me' (1 Cor. 11:17–34).

The Jews celebrate Purim, so named after the lot that Haman cast to seek an auspicious day for their destruction. The nature of that celebration can be gleaned from a contemporary Jewish website[1] that joyfully proclaims, 'Purim is the most festive of Jewish holidays, a time of prizes, noisemakers, costumes and treats. So here for your entertainment are some fun Holiday things for you and your family. We've got stories of Queen Esther, King Ahasuerus, Mordechai, and Haman, we've got graggers to spin, and Hamantashan to bake! We hope you find something you like!' It is a time for fun and the giving of presents.

The need to justify the institution of a new festival is evident. This feast was not ancient; nor did it have Mosaic authority. It was something that they had confessedly 'taken on themselves' [9:27] to ordain. Such exceptional action needed special pleading. There being evidently no precedent being set, this new festival is a one-off. It is not every day that the chosen people are delivered from annihilation by the mighty hand of God. There is no justification here for the later practice within branches of the professing church to fill the calendar with 'feasts, fasts and saints' days'.

It is a mark of the prestige and power of both Esther and Mordecai that they both issue decrees in the land of their exile and institute customs among the Jews.

Mordecai the great 10:1–3

After a brief recapitulation of the main events, the book closes with 'suggested further reading'. The deeds not only of Xerxes but also of Mordecai were apparently detailed in 'the annals of the kings of Media and Persia'. Sadly that volume is lost to us, but the inspired account has been, and will forever be, preserved by the hand of God.

Reflection/discussion topics from chapter 14

1 How can we fittingly mark the grace and mercy of God in our own lives?

2 Have you ever considered keeping a weekly spiritual journal or diary? Follow these directions:

In a typical week you could list the insights God has given you from your daily reading of Scripture.

- Record the truths you have enjoyed from midweek and Sunday ministry.
- List the matters for prayer leaving space to later record the answers.
- Record the things for which you have given thanks.
- Make a summary for prayer concerning some area of world Mission.[2]
- List the attributes of God you have come across and how they have affected your understanding of him and your relationship to him.
- Record brief details of opportunities for witness to remind you to pray.

- Take brief notes of lessons learnt from Christian books or magazines you are reading.

3 *Consider* Psalm 42. What does it teach us about the value of spiritual reflection?

4 The observance of any 'day' other than the Lord's Day is not commanded in Scripture (Col. 2:16). What value, if any, is there in keeping occasions such as Christmas, Easter and Harvest? What are the dangers? What are the advantages?

5 How can we help ourselves and each other to 'live by faith' (2 Cor. 5:7), bearing in mind that Esther, like Joseph, spent years in a difficult situation before the hand of the invisible God was seen to move. *Consider* Esther and Genesis 37, 39–47.

Notes

1 http://www.holidays.net/purim/

2 **Patrick Johnstone**'s book *Operation World* (Paternoster Publishing) is a goldmine for such information and magazines and fact sheets are easily obtained from most Mission Societies.

The festivals of Israel

Day of Atonement

Held on the 10th day of the 7th month.

Lev. 23:27, 16:29; Num. 29:7.

A solemn festival, including fasting, to remind Israel of her sin and the need for atonement

Dedication

Known as Hanukkah and the Feast of Lights.

John 10:22.

Developed in the time of the Maccabees to celebrate the cleansing of the Temple after its desecration by Antiochus Epiphanes.

Jubilee

Held every 50th year.

Lev. 23:15–16, 25:8–55, 27:14–24; Jer. 34:8, 14–17; Isa. 61:1–2.

It began with the blowing of the Ram's Horn Trumpet or Shofar. During that year Israelite slaves were set free and land returned to its ancestral owners.

New moon

Held each New Moon.

Exod. 40:2,17; Num. 10:10, 28:1–10,11–15; Ps. 104:19.

Offerings of two bullocks, one ram, seven lambs and one kid were made along with grain mixed with oil. A trumpet blast introduced this feast.

Passover

Observed on the 14th day of the first month, Abib, with the service beginning in the evening.

Exod. 12:1–13:16, 23:15, 34:18–20,25; Lev. 23:4–14; Num. 28:16–25; Deut. 16:1–8; Josh. 4:19–23, 5:10–12; 2 Chron. 30:2–3,13,15.

The Passover was the first of the three great festivals of the Israelite people. It celebrated the night when the people of Israel, slaves in Egypt, were delivered from the tenth plague by smearing the blood of the lamb on their doorposts so that the Angel of God would 'pass over' their houses when he destroyed all the firstborn of Egypt. The lamb was eaten with unleavened bread and bitter herbs. The people wore their outdoor clothes as if ready to depart.

Sabbath

Held weekly from the evening of each Friday to the evening of each Saturday. This ordinance, going back to creation, was included in the ten commandments given to Moses on Mount Sinai.

Exod. 16:22–30, 20:8–11, 23:12, 31:12–16, 34:21, 35:2–3; Lev. 23:3, 26:2; Num. 15:32–36, 28:9–10; Deut. 5:12–15.

Its literal meaning was 'to cease or abstain'. Given to commemorate God resting from his work of creation on the seventh day. It gained added significance after the exodus (Deut. 5:12–15) when it reminded Israel of its lengthy bondage (430 years) without any rest. No work was undertaken by man or beast on that day. In a way unlike any other festival the observance of the Sabbath set the Israelites apart from their neighbours. It is continued with new significance as the Christian Sunday, called the Lord's Day or the First Day of the week.

Seventh month festival

Held every 7th month.

Lev. 23:24–25,27–32; Num. 29:1–40.

Also known as the Feast of Trumpets it was commenced with the blowing of trumpets.

Feast of tabernacles or booths

Held on the 15th day of the seventh month to celebrate the completion of the autumn harvest.

Exod. 23:16; 34:22; Lev. 23:33–36,39–43; Num. 29:12–32; Deut. 16:13–16; Ezra 3:4; Zech. 14:16,18–19.

Features of the celebration included a holy 'assembly' on the first and eighth days, during which many animal sacrifices were offered. Israel was commanded to live in booths made of palm and willow trees to re-enact the period of wilderness wandering when they had no permanent dwellings.

Feast of weeks

Held early in the third month on the 50th day after barley sheaf was offered at the Feast of Unleavened Bread.

Exod. 23:16, 34:22; Lev. 23:15–21; Num. 28:26–31; Deut. 16:9–12; 2 Chron. 8:13.

Guests at the feast included servants, sons and daughters, Levites, the fatherless, the widow, and the stranger. This feast was also known as the Feast of Harvest or Pentecost (a Greek word meaning 'fifty'). It was the feast being celebrated when the gift of the Holy Spirit was poured out on the early church in fulfilment of the prophesy in Joel 2:28–31.

Feast of purim

Held annually on the 14th and 15th of Adar, it was named after the *Pur* or lot cast by Haman.

Only mentioned in Esth. 3:7, 9:24,26,28–29,31–32.

A time of great joy and celebration, eating drinking and exchanging of presents, it commemorates the deliverance of the Jews in the time of Xerxes, King of Persia, from the wicked plot of Haman the Agagite. It was instituted by Esther and Mordecai.

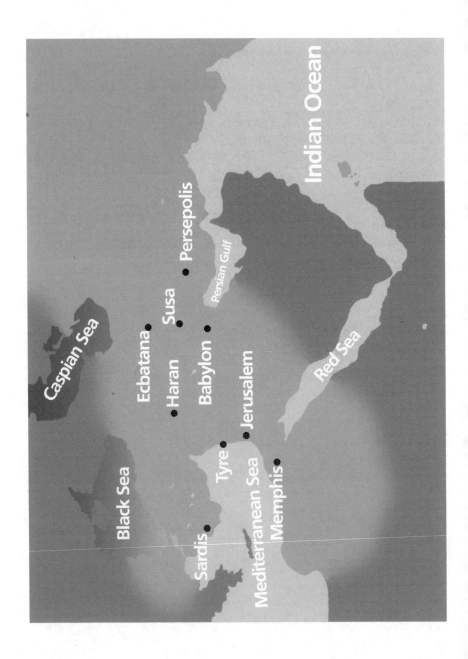

Notes

Notes

Notes